ABIDING

ABIDING

THE ARCHBISHOP OF CANTERBURY'S LENT BOOK 2013

BEN QUASH

BLOOMSBURY

LONDON • NEW DELHI • NEW YORK • SYDNEY

First published in Great Britain 2012

Copyright © Ben Quash, 2012

The moral right of the author has been asserted

No part of this book may be used or reproduced in any manner whatsoever without written permission from the Publishers except in the case of brief quotations embodied in critical articles or reviews. Every reasonable effort has been made to trace copyright holders of material reproduced in this book, but if any have been inadvertently overlooked the Publishers would be glad to hear from them.

A Continuum book

Bloomsbury Publishing Plc
50 Bedford Square
London WC1B 3DP

www.bloomsbury.com

Bloomsbury Publishing, London, New Delhi, New York and Sydney

Unless otherwise indicated, scripture quotations are taken from the New Revised Standard Version Bible, copyright 1989, Division of Christian Education of the National Council of the Churches of Christ in the United States of America. Used by permission. All rights reserved.

Scripture quotations from The Authorized (King James) Version, the rights of which are vested in the Crown, are reproduced by permission of the Crown's patentee, Cambridge University Press.

A CIP record for this book is available from the British Library.

ISBN 978 1 4411 5111 7

10 9 8 7 6 5 4 3 2 1

Typeset by Fakenham Prepress Solutions, Fakenham, Norfolk NR21 8NN

Printed and bound by CPI Group (UK) Ltd, Croydon, CRO 4YY

For my Godchildren,
with love and gratitude

Contents

FOREWORD BY THE ARCHBISHOP OF CANTERBURY

This is a reflection on where we find our centre of gravity. Ben Quash diagnoses with great sensitivity the different ways in which we can misunderstand our need for continuity and security – by resorting to inflexible habits or expectations, by looking for unchanging landmarks in a world where things naturally change, and equally by locating what really matters in an all-powerful individual will that ought to be able to mould reality according to its agenda. Against all this, he sets the habits of patience, the willingness to learn and be changed, the readiness to be someone else's guest and dependent, the renouncing of heroic fantasies in favour of ordinary sense and sensitivity and readiness to respond generously. This is a book about learning to inhabit your body and your history without resentment; it is also about inhabiting, steadily and mindfully, the daily disciplines of exposing yourself to the Bible and the rhythms of liturgical prayer. It celebrates the backgrounds and contexts we don't choose. It focuses our attention on attention itself, the kind of patient looking that Annie Dillard described, in the title of a famous book, as *Teaching a Stone to Talk*.

It is written with clarity and openness, introducing us to a good deal of painful personal experience without any jarring note of self-dramatising, and showing a wide range of interest in contemporary culture. Ben demonstrates very plainly the importance to Christian reflection of the riches found in modern fiction and film. At the same time, we are introduced to some of the major figures of the classical Christian tradition. St Benedict and his Rule feature prominently; but we also have a chance to become acquainted with a much less well-known figure from the fourth century, Macrina, sister of bishops and theologians who regarded her as their teacher and inspiration, the account of whose death is the subject of some of the most searching pages here.

Ben Quash has succeeded in holding together the uneasy and often bewildering plurality of the modern heart or mind with the depths of the tradition he inherits, both the Anglican inheritance and the wider legacy of early and mediaeval Christian thought and prayer. In this way he himself models the 'abiding', the letting-yourself-be-centred, that he analyses with such vividness and humanity. This is a large meditation in a small space – appropriate for us who live immortally in the local space of a fragile body.

+Rowan Cantuar

NOTE TO READERS

There is no obligation to read the chapters in this book in any particular order, or even, of course, to read them all. Each of them ought to make sense read on its own, even though some chapters have passing references to points or examples from other chapters. However, in constructing the book I have also had in mind the needs of individuals, groups or congregations who might want to read it in a systematic way during the weeks of Lent 2013. If you do want to use the book in this way, the approach most in line with its structure would be to read chapter 1, 'Abiding in Body', in the days between Ash Wednesday and the First Sunday of Lent; to read chapter 2, 'Abiding in Mind', in the week following the First Sunday of Lent, and then to read one chapter per week. This should mean that chapter 7, 'The Peace that Abides', will be read in the week following Passion Sunday. The short epilogue, 'Who May Abide?', can either be read at the same time as chapter 7, as a sort of extension of it (for those who will be quite busy enough as it is during Holy Week), or it can be reserved for Holy Week itself.

INTRODUCTION

A biding is not a word we have much use for in ordinary conversation. You wouldn't say, for example, 'oh, just abide here for a minute while I pop into the newsagents', or, 'she abode with me until the train arrived'. It is a word more suited to Victorian hymnody, along with phrases like 'fast falls the eventide'.

But it is not a word we can easily find substitutes for either, because 'wait' or 'stick around' don't quite catch it. Abiding has more the sense of a full, personal commitment. It expresses a quality of solidarity which just waiting would never convey; something like the widowed Ruth's wonderful words to her mother-in-law:

> Where you go, I will go; where you
> lodge, I will lodge; your people shall
> be my people, and your God my God.
> Where you die, I will die – there will I be
> buried. May the Lord do thus and so to
> me, and more as well, if even death parts
> me from you! (Ruth 1.16-17)

It is often remarked, lamentingly, that there is a strong tendency in our world not to *persevere* very much any more, and perhaps that is one of the reasons why the word 'abide' is dropping out of use. Various aspects of modern life contribute to the difficulty. Employment contracts tend to be temporary (meaning we don't feel deep personal loyalty to our employers or the institutions we belong to). The language of 'flexibility' has an unprecedentedly honoured place in the panoply of modern social virtues. And our deficiencies, our weaknesses, our wounds or our mistakes tend to be cover-uppable in a culture where we can select and present an image of ourselves and change it at will, denying that the self we *have been* has any real continuity with the self we are *now*.

The challenge of finding the right ways to be an abider in such a world is huge. It's the challenge of finding the source from which our life flows, the spring of our own being, the grain with which we are meant to live, and which it damages us to go against. It means being part of communities for whom 'abiding' is a watchword – above all, for Christians, the Church.

This book is intended to help Christians think about those challenges, and how best to live lives that address – with boldness and imagination – the difficulties of abiding under the very particular pressures of today's world.

But it is also a book that wants to complicate its main category a little. Because Christian abiding is not (i) the same as keeping things just as they always have been, nor is it always (ii) the same as sheer staying power.

Flexibility may be over-prized in contemporary capitalist culture, but a near cousin of the virtue of perseverance is *stubbornness,* and that would be no very welcome alternative to flexibility in a Christian perspective. In the language of the Bible, 'wicked' often also implies 'stiff-necked'.[1]

It may be tempting to lament a decline in modern people's power of abiding, but under the surface most people are still, in the end, quite conservative. They like the things they know; they like their routines; they like their home environments. In such instincts we can see that an inclination to abide is perhaps as strong in people as ever. But this is not exactly the Christian abiding that Jesus modelled for his first followers, when he lived with nowhere to lay his head, and asked them to leave everything and follow him. There is something strange and unsettling for the more conservatively-minded person about Jesus's message of discontinuity and dispossession.

On the other hand, he wasn't recommending the spiritual equivalent of extreme 'wilderness survival' either. Those who feel claustrophobic when faced with the conservatism that just wants to maintain the status quo can be tempted to a radical rupture with the existing order of things which is – often – a sort of self-assertion. They carve out their own path; they do it their way, through thick and thin. *Their* form of abiding is their *staying power*. But this steely exercise of the individual will is not what Jesus taught any more than inertia is. He asked people to surrender their wills, to recognize their dependencies, and above all to exchange individual autonomy for 'eccentric existence'[2] – life in, with, and through others, in the community of the Church.

So there is a conundrum at the heart of this book, which I hope will generate some energy for Christian thinking and also for Christian living. It is between the centrality to the Christian outlook of order, consistency and continuity, on the one hand, and the equal centrality of relinquishment, openness and change, on the other. There is no doubt that Christians are called to abide as Jesus abides, who in his abiding shows us how to relate well to God. But this abiding won't be the achievement of the solitary will, and it will take us off the edges of our familiar maps and into uncharted territories where we find that abiding (when it is *abiding-in-God*) will also mean transformation and relationships we cannot wholly control.

Each of the book's chapters begins by introducing a character to the reader. Some of these are fictional and some are historical. The hope in introducing them is that they will offer a vivid way into some of the themes that the chapter will go on to explore (usually by illustrating some form of abiding, though occasionally by being a negative image of it), and that they will be guardians against the tendency theology sometimes has to become too concept-driven and dry.

Literature, film and other forms of the arts are instructors in how to make ideas *thoroughly incarnate*, to echo an insight of the novelist George Eliot,[3] and if Christian theology has failed to do the same in the way it presents *its* ideas, it has failed absolutely. (This is, incidentally, one of the reasons why theology's relationship with the arts needs to be nurtured and prized.) I hope these characters are not a source of irritation, and that (if you haven't already) you enjoy meeting them.

At the end of each chapter there is a 'Coda' that suggests a topic of reflection and relates it to a text from one of the readings set in the Common Worship lectionary for one of the weeks between Ash Wednesday and Easter Sunday.

Rowan Williams, who commissioned this book, is one of the best examples I know of what it means to abide; with profound patience he has dwelt with and in a Church that has been finding it hard to abide with itself, and in its concern with issues of unity, catholicity and apostolicity he has been a constant reminder to it of its call to holiness. I am enduringly grateful for him, for his example, and for his invitation to write this book.

I should like to acknowledge the many people – family and friends and colleagues – whose love, insight and forbearance provided the conditions without which this book could not have been produced. I should especially like to acknowledge some people with whom I have an abiding relationship in the communion of the Church. It is a precious relationship that I did not get by some contract or by any process of nature, but by grace:

> Springing from the freedom
> Of the daring, trusting spirit...[4]

They are Harry Carleton Paget, Eleanor Dowler, Daniel Ford, Lucy Heaton, Eleanor Kashouris, Miranda Musson, Isabel Shephard, Anna Wilson, and Martha Zemmrich. I thank God for them and the many things I receive from them.

1
ABIDING IN BODY

The character with whom I want to begin this chapter is a monk. He lived from around 480 to 547 AD in central and then in southern Italy. He was so hugely admired by Gregory I, who was Pope some 50 years after he died, that Gregory wrote a tribute to him, based on the recollections of other monks who had known him. It may not meet today's expectations of what a biography should be, but it is the earliest account of that monk's disciplined but humane life that we have to go on, and it permits us to conjure him up as a very young man of about 20, quitting his studies in Rome and setting off into mountainous country to embrace the vocation of a hermit.

He chose a cave at the head of a valley with a lake in it. We can picture him picking his way along the valley's steep sides, past the ruins of ancient Roman glories: a palace that had once been Nero's, a grand complex of baths, and a 25-arch bridge connecting them. Amidst the debris of a world order that had collapsed, he was willing to start building again. Some of the words set by the lectionary for reading on Ash Wednesday capture what might have been this monk's hope. They are God's words to the Jewish exiles returning to Jerusalem from Babylon: 'your ancient ruins shall be rebuilt; you shall raise up the foundations of many generations; you shall be called the repairer of the breach, the restorer of streets to live in' (Isaiah 58.12).

The monk was, of course, Benedict – later St Benedict – whose three years in that cave would prepare him for a life founding and living in small communities under a shared rule of life.

Benedict would also in time, and by a much later Pope, be named patron saint and protector of Europe. It could do with his patronage now. As I am writing this, the turmoil in the Eurozone threatens the stability of the world economy yet again. It seems likely that we are witnessing the beginning of a significant decline in the influence, economic status, and quality of life of Western European countries – if not of the West more widely. The sorts of political instability that may follow such a decline are hard to predict, but are certain to be considerable. Meanwhile, big global flows of population (already a volatile feature of our world) look likely to continue, and these too create their own kinds of instability.

Forces and movements on this scale can sometimes seem very far removed from the local spaces in which human beings try to live meaningfully, yet their effects can rip devastatingly through people's lives. The circumstances that determine how much someone's pension will be worth in five years' time are as unpredictable and as out of our control as the strains of new virus that seem able to pop up in any corner of the world at any moment and find their way to any doorstep in a matter of weeks.

How can stable lives be lived in a world like this? This is where the figure of Benedict continues to be instructive, for it was a similar question that he faced 1500 years ago. As the ruins he looked down upon from his cave would have proclaimed daily, *his* Europe was in a state of collapse, as an old order (that of the Christian Roman Empire) gave way to a fragmented and dangerous new one. The flows of population tended to be violent ones, as warlike tribes swept southwards across

Italy destroying much of what was in their path (including – after his death – the monastery that Benedict would eventually found at Monte Cassino). There was precipitous economic decline in Benedict's lifetime. Plague was a constant threat and poverty was a daily presence.

Benedict's *Rule* – modelled on some existing patterns of monastic life that already had a long pedigree in both the western and the eastern Church, but adding some special ingredients of his own – was his hopeful and constructive response to the uncertainties of his time. It was to become the most influential paradigm of monastic living there has ever been. Indeed, as one admirer remarks, it is 'surely the oldest written constitution under which twentieth-century men and women are still living'.[1]

It's a familiar fact that the vows under which most monks and nuns live are the threefold ones of poverty, chastity and obedience – and Benedict's monks certainly lived lives in which all these three disciplines would have been very central. But the actual *vows* they made (and that Benedictines today still make) were obedience, conversion, and *stability*. The vow of stability requires professed monks to stay in the houses where they make their profession. In a few cases – for some exceptional reason – they may be transferred to another house, or seconded to perform a role somewhere else that serves the wider Church, but otherwise they stay in their 'home' community until they die. Benedict did not invent the idea that stability was important, but he made it the *typical* feature of the monastic tradition he founded. It is the one vow that is always mentioned in the various early versions of his *Rule* that survive, even though other elements sometimes aren't there. It is, you might say, the *sine qua non* of the Benedictine spirit, and the essential ingredient of a Benedictine profession. So it is worth asking what the nature of this stability was, and what purpose it was meant to serve.

First and foremost, it expresses a commitment to the importance of *community*, and more particularly communities of diverse people whose diversity anticipates the Kingdom of God (more of this shortly). But second – and for the sake of such community – the vow of stability expresses a commitment to *place*. Christian societies like those Benedict founded can only be durable societies if they are embedded in particular, dedicated places. And third, the vow of stability expresses a commitment to *education*, or *formation*, in such embedded and durable communities. So the stability that a follower of Benedict promises to embrace is a willingness to abide *somewhere*, because this will enable an abiding with a particular group of *someones*, and this in turn is important because it will enable a certain sort of transformative abiding with God and oneself.

I called this chapter, which is about stability, 'Abiding in Body' for the sake of a contrast with the chapter that comes after it, which will be about contemplation, and is called 'Abiding in Mind'. But it is an artificial distinction of course, because as all good Christian teaching insists, human minds are always embodied minds, and human bodies are intellectual bodies. The *Rule* of Benedict already makes this clear in the way it coordinates the advantages of being somewhere bodily with *learning*, which is an activity of body and mind together. The '*enclosure*' of the monastery (its physical parameters) provides the necessary conditions for that special sort of *community* which can also be a '*school*'. As Benedict puts it, if we want to obtain eternal life then 'while we are in this body and there is time to carry out all these things by the light of this life, we must [...] found a school for the Lord's service'.[2] The external aspects of a boundaried place are not incidental and dispensable to this. They are foundational to the way in which Benedict's monks – in their chaotic, poor, dangerous and plague-ridden world – were able to come into an intimate relationship with God, and a truthful relationship with themselves. Life in community was the middle term that translated one into the other – that allowed being in a location to serve life with God.

Benedict's *Rule* is clear that alternative models of monastic life that are based on peripatetic wandering have a high risk of being corrupted. He has a name for monks of this sort – the 'gyrovagues' – who 'spend their whole lives lodging in different regions and different monasteries three or four days at a time, always wandering and never stable, serving their own wills and the lure of gluttony...'

Gyrovagues are not like the friars of later mendicant orders (Franciscans and Dominicans, for instance) who are part of an organized body

15

and live under the discipline of a rule even though they move from location to location. Gyrovagues are 'freelance' monks, who go where they please and subsist on the resources of institutions to which they do not belong. With stability neither in a place nor in a community they are vulnerable to the temptations of boredom or disenchantment (the technical Latin term for this vice was '*acedia*') – temptations that make the grass seem always greener on the other side of the fence; temptations that beckon them towards alternatives that seem certain to offer a better answer, or a more complete satisfaction. The gyrovagues are, we might say, truants from the school of stability. The monk who commits to community, says Benedict, is by contrast 'a very strong kind of monk'.[3]

Benedict's *Rule* with its emphasis on stability can easily fuel a complaint about the ills of our fast and fluid modern world, because our world's ways seem so at odds with the Benedictine spirit. Michael Paternoster writes:

> More and more people are obliged to change jobs and houses every few years, never settling and putting down roots.

> We can, I think, legitimately criticize a
> society so organized that mobility on
> this scale has begun to efface the older
> pattern of stable community life...

This makes a powerful point, and it is close to the heart of much of what this book wants to argue – although (as we will also see) the complaint can too easily translate into a call for greater moral strenuousness (more *effort*), an endeavour which the Reformation churches could swiftly have identified as 'works-righteousness', and St Augustine of Hippo (a thousand years before) might have suspected of being 'Pelagian' (for a description of what the Pelagian heresy was, see p.85 in Chapter 3). Paternoster doesn't go down this route – he adds the important qualification that 'we cannot blame the people who find themselves travelling on this merry-go-round' for their failures to put down deep roots.[4] A 'merry-go-round' world makes it well-nigh impossible for people to stabilize themselves even if they want to, and individual decisions are not enough to stop the carousel turning.

But *collectively* there are ways in which something different can be fostered and sustained, especially perhaps in the community of the Church, a community – so I have claimed – whose watchword is abiding. Benedict's hopeful and constructive response to his fragmented times was communitarian. He didn't just tell people to abide, he gave them a context for abiding: a place and a pattern. Without this, they would never have been able to withstand the onslaughts of their turbulent age and grow in holiness.

Some recent critics of the 'Fresh Expressions' movement in the Church, spawned by the Church of England's 2004 report *Mission-Shaped Church*,[5] articulate the importance of place in a way that has a great deal in common with Benedict's insistence on stability. 'Our country is crying out for a rebirth of locality', they exclaim, as they defend the parish system with its commitment to geographical presence and coverage.[6] Their celebration of the role of the parish church has a number of aspects, but two key ones are the following. First of all, the parish church is a long-term institution: it *abides in time*. Indeed:

> [it] is committed to the longest possible time-scale. It intends to be in the

community as long as the community exists.[7]

And the corollary of this is that it also *abides in place* – this is the second key virtue of the parish.

There are kinds of community that I can choose to belong to because they are full of people like me, or of people with the same interests as me. Sports teams, Facebook groups, book clubs all have this aspect to them – and perform a valuable function in my life. But they are only as stable as my interests. If I drop one hobby in favour of another, or switch my sporting allegiances or my reading habits, I will probably change the community in whose company I pursue my interest. This is emphatically not Benedictine-style stability; that's to say, it is not the sort of stability that could sustain the sort of community that changes *me* as opposed to the sort of community that *I can exchange*. It is the way of the modern-day gyrovague.

The Church, as Benedict knew, is the sort of community that transforms its members. This may happen imperceptibly over a lifetime but it transforms them nonetheless – and that it

19

happens over a lifetime is exactly the point. The Church is not an interest group, and its members do not come together because they are all like each other (or even because they like each other) but because they believe that they are all God's redeemed children. If they try to walk away from each other, they will meet each other again at the foot of the Cross, through which Christ has broken down the barriers between his children and made them all one (whether they like it or not).

The risk of some Fresh Expressions is that they are communities which people have opted into rather than found themselves present to. Place is not their starting point, and if you take *place* out of the equation it is prone to being replaced by a more naked sort of *choice*. A community of free association is only as stable its members' inclination to associate, and it will not necessarily transform its members very much. A community of Benedictine embeddedness is as stable as the place and pattern of life which make it an anticipation of the Kingdom, and it can transform its members *a lot*.

The Kingdom is not homogeneous. Similarly, although we make choices about where to live, any given locality is rarely full of people who are of like mind. This means that given localities can be signs of the Kingdom of God. '[T]he mixed community of the parish church is our local witness to the Church as mixed, universal and all embracing,' write Andrew Davison and Alison Milbank.[8] The Church is an almost miraculous body in this respect.

The occasions on which we come together regularly to express a fellowship – a covenantal bond – with a range of people utterly unlike ourselves are very few in number. The local church is to be treasured because it signifies the wholeness of the humanity God is drawing to redeemed completeness; it is, you might say, 'the true universal community in embryo'.[9]

In Benedict's own time – and throughout the medieval period – the *Rule* was a rare and powerful antidote to social stratification; paradoxically, its special sort of stability was 'a powerful force for social *fluidity*' in European history.[10] This was because your class origins, your former wealth, and even your age made no difference to your seniority in the monastery: the only measure of seniority was how long you had been in the house. In this respect too, the community's equal regard for all was a foretaste of the heavenly realm.

And this brings us back to a key insight of Benedict's *Rule*. We have already seen how enclosure (place) grounds the sort of community that can be a 'school' capable of preparing its members for eternal life. Only a community of the diverse can be educative like that – knocking one's edges off, and helping one to learn more about the God of the whole world by seeing how various its occupants are.

A closely related piece of wisdom is encoded in the way that stability relates to the other two Benedictine vows: that of obedience and that of conversion of one's habits. In a sense stability is the condition of both. Obedience is meant to have conversion of life as its proper outcome (it is what the 'school' of the Benedictine community is *for*); you cannot have transformation without obedience. But you cannot learn obedience to anything or anyone other than yourself if you cannot stay still; if you are constantly in thrall to an itch for the new. Benedict's *Rule* is designed to encourage its readers to stick with it when things get difficult and they are inclined to give up or go somewhere else. In chapter 58, other words occur alongside the key word *stabilitas* (which in fact occurs only six times in the *Rule*) and these may help us to appreciate other ideas to which the idea of stability is related. The chapter discusses how a community is to decide whether or not to receive a new member. Easy entry is not to be granted. The newcomer must show *perseverance*, they must show *patience*, they must show *persistence* (all these words appear in the space of just a few lines), and they must *abide*. The Latin word here is '*stare*'; it can also be translated 'standing firm', 'remaining' or simply 'staying'. Only by manifesting these qualities does a would-be monk show himself ready for life in community.

The chapter talks of a series of time periods that the newcomer will have to pass in the enclosure, and different disciplines he must be introduced to, with this recurring refrain (using the abide-word '*stare*'): 'if he still stays... and if he still stays... and if...'[11] Only then can he be received into the community.

Interestingly, the third vow – which is often taken to be a promise to embrace 'conversion' of one's ways – is probably even better rendered

23

'conversation'. It is a strange phrase, echoing the hard-to-translate line in Paul's Letter to the Philippians which the King James Bible renders: 'our conversation is in heaven' (Philippians 3.20).

The original Greek word in Philippians is *politeuma*, which modern versions translate as 'citizenship'. In Benedict's *Rule*, 'conversation' (*conversatio* in Latin) is meant to suggest transformation every bit as much as 'conversion' does, but it has the advantage of emphasizing the fact that there is nothing instantaneous about being made fit for holiness; in fact, it is very much a kind of citizenship. 'Conversion' often suggests a single moment of change; this, on the other hand, is a process that never ends – a process of transformative *abiding*.

Parish communities, like Benedictine monasteries, offer people the gift of a certain sort of stability, and this gift of stability (this gift of a *pattern* in a *place*) can be an extraordinary resource for a person's formation along with other people as citizens of heaven. Parishes, like stable Benedictine houses, proclaim the fact that 'the Christian life can all be done on the spot', as Monica Furlong puts it.[12] Of course, there are differences between parishes and monasteries. Benedictine houses are 'total communities' of the sort that are few and far between today – communities in which work, rest, study and prayer are all shared with the same people in the same place. Modern people frequently work at some distance from their homes, and spend their leisure time in a variety of locations too. But that ought not to lead to an overstatement of the 'virtual' or 'placeless' character of choice-governed modern existence. There are still many 'givens' in our lives – our neighbours, work colleagues and families are not people we have 'opted for' to any vastly greater extent today than we did at any time in the past, and they remain fundamental to the fabric of our daily existence.

It is not an accident that parishes have so much in common with Benedictine communities, for (in England at least) one of the profoundest influences on Church life has been the Benedictine spirit – a spirit that we can see at work as far back as the mission to reclaim Britain for Christianity that was led by St Augustine of Canterbury at Pope Gregory's behest in 596 AD.

The Venerable Bede (672/673–735), who wrote down the story of this mission, used it as an opportunity to articulate the distinctive genius of English Christianity, and he did so from the point of view of someone living under the Benedictine *Rule*, which had been adopted by his communities at Jarrow and at Wearmouth.

He shows us that Augustine and his fellow missionary monks didn't only found cloisters and schools; they established parishes, dioceses and provinces. As a consequence, the monastic presence extended to the very heart of the Church diocese:

> Many monks subsequently became bishops, and England developed the curious custom, elsewhere practically unknown, of the 'Cathedral priory' where the cathedral of a diocese was manned not by secular clerks but by professed monks. About half of the great cathedral churches in England were monastic, the prior and monks taking the place of the dean and canon.[13]

It was a spirit that was more adapted than it was extinguished at the time of the English Reformation. Even though the priors and monks have gone, a monastic pattern of prayer and communal existence in an enclosure (or 'close') is still a feature of the life of English cathedral clergy today. And the *Book of Common Prayer*, which was to become the primary spiritual source-book for Anglicans (a book of liturgy rather than any confessional codification of doctrine), holds on tightly to the idea that a (very Benedictine) shared pattern of daily prayer, the reading of Scripture, and participation in the eucharist is at the core of Anglican identity.

Anglican morning and evening prayer are a distillation of the monastic offices so that they can be used in parishes by any Christian man or woman; it is not a rejection of the Benedictine pattern, so much as a new dissemination of it.

Peter Anson (a Roman Catholic) and A. W. Campbell (an Anglican), in their classical study of religious communities in the Anglican Communion, note that the Anglican Church as such is thus a kind of generalized monastic community.[14] This is even true of its global structure and its model of Church authority, for Benedictine houses have largely seen themselves as more a worldwide network of local and regional presences, rather than spokes radiating from a central hub.

I can imagine a sceptical reader thinking that my advocacy of the parish, and the celebration of the spirit of medieval monasticism which lies behind it, reveals a certain nostalgic roman-ticism for a bygone era. Hasn't the influence of the parish church faded from modern life along with the village bobbie and maypoles? I don't think that is a right assumption. Indeed, the parish church could be poised for a sort of prophetic (and encouraging) reminder to a creaking western world that local cooperation and community are still part of the art of the possible.

Perhaps its doubters assume that parish commu-nities are simply *beneficiaries* of times of cultural stability – part of a stability that they do not themselves create – and that when our culture enters periods of instability they are inevitably weakened. But, like Benedict's first communities, I think that parishes can be seen as *generators* of stability, whose purpose and value becomes even more visible when their environments are threatened. They abide. Their disciplines of

28

abiding enable them to give to their environments in a great Benedictine tradition, that of *hospitality*.

You cannot give hospitality without stability – without a place from which to offer it. Parishes are uniquely poised to be hospitable to their environments, to tend the public spaces they serve, to 'curate' them (which is to say, to preserve and interpret them for the common good, as curators in galleries and museums preserve and interpret the things they hold in trust for the general public). They can give meaning and identity to communities.

Part of my reason for believing this to be true is personal, and is the consequence of seeing the parish function in a context as difficult and as hostile as those that Benedict's first foundations encountered.

In 1990, newly-graduated from university, I went at the invitation of a South African priest (whom I had met by chance on a rickety tour bus in the Holy Land) to spend eight months living and working in the Western Townships of Johannesburg as a lay parish assistant. In the

nomenclature of the apartheid regime, it was an
area designated for 'coloureds' to live in (that is,
people of mixed race, who lived alongside those
of Indian extraction), merging on its western side
into the black townships of Soweto. I wanted to
explore what I felt might be a vocation to the
priesthood, and hoped to experience Anglicanism
in a radically different context. When I arrived
in South Africa, the apartheid laws that made it
technically illegal for me to live in a non-white
area of the city were still on the statute books
– though they were only to remain there for
another few months. It was a country on the
brink of a huge transition.

That time in South Africa exposed me to an instability I had never experienced before, but with a
strange simultaneity showed me a stability that
was new as well. I had no idea where I would be
living for those eight months, and it turned out
that no one else did either until the day I arrived
at the airport. My new friend Justus, the priest
who had asked me out to work with him, had
approached a local family only that morning to
ask if they would give me a room in their house.
Fortunately they said yes, and so I found myself
in the spare bedroom of Mr and Mrs Baker's

house with three generations of their family inside it, and four Rottweilers patrolling the small yard at the back.

It was hard ever to feel entirely safe. The Rottweilers were threatening enough, but it quickly became apparent that their presence there was itself a response to wider threats beyond the perimeter. When I walked the half mile through the township to the parish church each morning to pray the morning office, I was told to carry a stick because dogs in the houses along the way were trained to attack strangers. When I walked home in the evening, I would pass groups of migrant workers gathered around makeshift braziers outside the shuttered and barred local shop. At night – pretty much every night – I would hear the sounds of gunshots in the township: most likely gang warfare between drug traffickers, I was told, rather than political violence.

Two weeks into my time there, a group of men came to the Rectory – regular members of the church congregation – proposing to put a stop to a series of break-ins to the church premises which had resulted in people's harvest festival donations being stolen. They planned to keep guard in the

31

church all night. Justus was worried that the men would not be safe – what if the burglars were armed and violent? 'Then we'll shoot them, Father', came the reply.

Justus did not give them permission to occupy the church, and they didn't shoot anyone, but I was very rattled by what that episode revealed about the fragile circumstances in which human community was struggling to hold itself together in that place. It was a long way from the rural Wye Valley, on the border between England and Wales, where my teenage home and schooling had been. Another young man from England, who would also later be ordained priest and remains one of my closest friends, was at work in another area of the townships that sprawled for miles around. Together, we visited some of the shanty towns where the very poorest lived – using refuse to cobble together makeshift houses on the bare earth.

We spent an afternoon trying to hang a door between two pieces of corrugated iron while the family prepared a meal from a sheep's head salvaged from a butcher's garbage bin – scorching off the outer hair on a small fire, and then boiling it. It was an uncomfortable place to be: the shanty towns were home to kangaroo courts which administered rough justice – including that infamous punishment known as 'necklacing' which involved placing a rubber tyre over the offending person's head and setting fire to it. The Baragwanath Hospital in Soweto, where we made visits to give sick communions, often had patients who had been victims of machete attacks or who had been thrown off moving trains or buses.

Each of these encounters with a (to me) shocking unpredictability was accompanied by an experience of community and fellowship – or, to put it another way, by an experience of things that abided, and continue to abide. The shanty town where the threat of necklacing hung like a pall was also the place where I was met with one of the warmest welcomes I have ever had. A tradition of hospitality was strong.

The family who were asked – almost at random – to be *my* family for 8 months on the very morning that I arrived have remained something more than friends; 23 years later, I am still Mrs Baker's 'English son', and she is my other mother. And the township, with all its dogs and gunshots, sustained an extraordinary community life to which the church was central – its pattern of life generating a stability that Benedict would have recognized. The daily office and the eucharist were at the heart of its life; the Choir and a whole range of church fellowship groups – even the men's gathering for whisky, curry and cards – drew life from this heart.

What I conclude from this is that Benedictine-style stability, working through place and pattern, can withstand many pressures, and makes sense to people in very many different contexts. That's not to say that such stability is some sort of natural human state that will always assert itself whatever the adverse conditions. Parodic alternatives to such stability can offer themselves temptingly, and (like all evils) have an alluring similarity to the good from which they are a departure.

The apartheid regime was itself an attempt to assert a certain sort of stability – a static stability in which everyone would know their place, and each race could (supposedly) pursue its own development in its own way and at its own pace. It was a way of trying to fix, order and tidy up the world. But there are smaller versions of such fake stability than a great big political ideology like apartheid. South Africa in 1990 also exposed me for the first time to the phenomenon of *gated communities* – another sort of controlled and regulated environment that is now increasingly familiar in the UK too. These initiatives mistake security for stability. Security works by exclusion, invigilation and the management of risk. Stability, at least as Benedict conceived it, is oriented to openness, gift-giving and service. Security is for the benefit only of those inside the enclosure. Stability is as much for those outside as those within.

This is ultimately, as we have seen, because stability is intended to witness to our common humanity under God. It is about accepting rather than choosing one's neighbour, and giving people resources to belong to one another more fully than they might initially be inclined to do. It is, as one early Christian writer put it, a virtue we have 'in common with God', because it is an imitation of the divine patience:

> From Him patience begins; from Him its
> glory and its dignity take their rise. The

35

origin and greatness of patience proceed
from God as its author.[15]

To be in the presence of this patient God is to be
in the most perfectly stable dwelling place there
is. And this is perhaps why the introduction to
Benedict's *Rule* has so much to say about that
dwelling place – longing for it with eager passion:

> [L]et us ask the Lord, along with the
> prophet, saying to him, 'Lord, who will
> live in your dwelling place and who
> rests on your holy mountain?' After this
> question, brothers, let us hear the Lord in
> reply, showing us the way to his dwelling
> place, saying, [...] It is they who, fearing
> the Lord, do not puff themselves up
> for their good observance, but instead
> judging that the good in them cannot be
> created by themselves but by the Lord,
> glorify the Lord working in them, saying
> this with the prophet: 'not to us, Lord,
> not to us, but to your name give the
> glory'...[16]

This patience and generosity are God's, but
Christian disciples have a task of self-preparation

to perform nonetheless. As Benedict adds, it is still 'up to us to fulfill the dweller's duties'. This will mean being nurtured in our imitation of the divine patience, and finding the right ways to be stable – the right ways to live well in God's presence.

The patterns and places that ensure the sort of stability that is genuinely godly are hard-won patterns in precious places. They need to be sustained, defended and renewed in each generation. When they are lost, then it is a hard task to build them again from scratch, as Benedict knew. But when they endure, they can bear amazing fruit.

In the townships, I found myself giving sick communion regularly to a woman who was 100 years old, and lay all day on a bed in the corner of a tiny sitting room with her family running in and out and all around her. One day, she described her memories of being a girl of around 10 and taking food to British soldiers in red coats who were hiding out in caves. I suddenly realized that she was recalling the Boer War. Her eucharistic communion in the Church had been the accompaniment to a life of – to me – almost unimaginable length in which the world had undergone two World Wars, the splitting of the atom, the moon landings, not to mention the beginning and now the end of apartheid. A sort of 'eucharistic heartbeat' had been the abiding accompaniment to this long life. It was the fruit of a stability that the Church had maintained for her, as it does for countless others. It had helped prepare her for that dwelling place in God's Kingdom which was the object of Benedict's excited anticipation.

Coda

Rowan Williams wrote in *The Times* newspaper on Christmas Eve 2011 about a trip he had made to Eastern Congo in which he met thirty or so young men and women ('out of several hundred thousand across the globe') who had been forced into becoming child soldiers.

They had escaped, and were being helped, despite many setbacks and the psychological and physical wounds they had sustained, to become part of civilian life again. 'They had been brought out of the bush, prised out of the grip of the militias that had captured them and reintroduced to something like normality.'

How had it happened? They all had one
answer. The Church had not given up
on them. At great risk, members of local
Christian communities had kept contact
with them, sometimes literally gone in
search of them, helped them escape and
organised a return to civilian life. They
had prepared congregations to receive
them, love them and gradually get them
back into ordinary human relationships.

The message was always the same: 'they didn't
give up on us'. One challenge for Christians to
think about during Lent might be how better to
be communities and individuals whose presence
in a place provokes that sort of tribute – and
the sort of transformation that can give rise to
it. Parish communities, as Rowan Williams goes
on to say, did this in the UK at the time of the
summer riots in 2011. They turned out 'to put
themselves at the service of all that was best in
communities'. They were 'the people who were
relied on to pick up the pieces in any number of
ways'.

They could do it because they were trusted. And
they were trusted because local communities

knew they were not going to go away and give up. They were abiding communities, and it is this abiding that 'makes the change that matters'.

'Gather the people. Sanctify the congregation', says Joel in one of the readings set for Ash Wednesday (Joel 2.16). Think about your community – your place – this Lent. Think about a way in which you might show your commitment to it; might help to 'curate' it. You might adorn it in some way. You might tidy it. You might find a way to gather some of the people in it. These are all ways to serve your place and to sanctify it – and to show that you do not intend to give up on it.

'You shall raise up the foundations of many generations; you shall be called the repairer of the breach, the restorer of streets to live in' (Isaiah 58.12).

2
ABIDING IN MIND

Let one set of ruins – those that St Benedict picked his way through in order to begin his hermit life – give way to another. Imagine a ruined amphitheatre, on the outskirts of a town. As the town's busy life has moved on, as the generations have come and gone, its inhabitants have almost completely forgotten about the amphitheatre, which lies hidden in a little pine wood to the south of the town. A few professors of ancient history know about it, but they never visit it any more because it holds nothing more for them to research. In a place that was once filled with human performers and human listeners, the song of the cicadas is the only sound. It is deserted.

Until, one day, mysteriously, a child appears from no-one-knows-where and takes up residence in the ruins. She is of indeterminate age – perhaps about 12 – and she has bare feet and wild, uncombed hair. She has a patchwork skirt and an oversized man's jacket with lots of pockets in it. Her name is Momo.

This latter-day solitary, unlike St Benedict, is a fictional character: the marvellous creation of the German writer Michael Ende, who first published her story in the 1970s.[1] The people of the region initially find her strange – she was, writes Ende, 'a little shocking to people who valued cleanliness and order'. But very quickly they come to love her and depend on her. Their care is expressed both in the gifts and supplies they bring her (for she owned nothing but what she found or was given) and in their efforts to make her dwelling place in the ruin more habitable, by setting her up with tables, chairs and a little oven to keep her warm in winter. Their dependency on her, meanwhile, grows in response to an extraordinary gift that she has.

The gift is not a magic power – though its results sometimes seem magical. Nor is it some very exotic skill or talent. It is the ability to listen. 'Only very few people can *really* listen', remarks the narrator. Momo can do it like no other; she listens with complete attentiveness and sympathy. (She also speaks extremely rarely.) The effect of this ability to listen is that people from all around come to talk to her – or perhaps more accurately, to talk in her presence, while she listens. Her listening awakens their speech, and it flows out from them, meaning that she is very rarely without some visitor sitting with her and talking. Some of the old purpose of the amphitheatre is revived, but in a reversed way, for whereas theatre comes alive when a body of people congregate to perform a collective act of *listening* while just a few people (and sometimes only one) *speak*, in Momo's theatre she is the one-person audience to the host of speakers who come and go.

Something comparable goes on when children come to the amphitheatre to play, which they begin to do daily. Momo simply makes herself available to join in with the games they suggest; her attentiveness and sympathy are put at the disposal of their ideas, so to speak, and the consequence of this is that their ideas come pouring out and they are never bored.

Her powers extend to non-human creatures too. A small boy brings his canary to Momo because it won't sing. Momo sits and listens to it for a whole week until finally it begins to trill and bubble with song again. On clear, starry nights, the narrator tells us, Momo sometimes sits in the middle of the amphitheatre beneath the star-strewn heavens and feels as though she is sitting cupped within a huge ear, which tunes her to a soft and yet powerful music in the spheres that speak strangely to her heart.

Momo is the character in whose company I want to begin this chapter because she represents a special sort of attentiveness, to all that is around (and above) her. She has what the poet Geoffrey Hill calls a heightened 'pitch of attention'.[2] Simone Weil (1909–43), in her classic book *Waiting for God*, described such generous concentration in a very similar way.[3]

Momo's quality of *listening* is a power that any reader of her story can aspire to share with her, and I think that her capacity for attention could just as well inspire a better attitude to *looking*. Both listening and looking can be forms of contemplation, which is the theme of this chapter.

When we contemplate, we become absorbed in the object that we are contemplating, and commune with it in a certain way. Our minds achieve a power of penetration in the mode of contemplation. It is important to reiterate here what was said in the previous chapter, that concentrating on 'Abiding in Body' and then moving on to 'Abiding in Mind' should not obscure the fact that both are always active together; each always implies the other. So Momo's actively sympathetic mind is bound up intrinsically with her highly attuned ears and her big, wide-open eyes. She contemplates the people who come to her in the same way she contemplates the stars in the sky at night – almost as though they are a work of art – and she needs a body as well as a mind in order to do it. But her physically being there issues nonetheless in an extraordinary level of thoughtful attention, and that quality of thoughtful attention, in its relevance for Christians, is going to be the focus of what follows.

Indeed, the main substance of this chapter will concern itself with one very *particular* focus for the contemplative activity of Christian minds, and that is the Bible. This is partly to continue in the Benedictine spirit of Chapter 1, because the Benedictine tradition places at the centre of its life of stability-in-a-place a practice of contemplatively reading Scripture. It *abides* with Scripture, studying it prayerfully. Shortly, in what follows, I will suggest a series of loosely related ways in which contemporary Christians might revive the contemplative intensity of their own reading of the Bible.

Many of the ways in which modern church-goers read or relate to Scripture are far from contemplative. Even Bible Study is too often not really *study*, or at least not the sort of study a Benedictine would recognize: one marked first and foremost by a kind of expectant attention, a spiritual 'listening', from which the religious understanding of obedience derives its real meaning. It is not study like Momo's studied concentration on those who visit her, and her studied interest in what they say. The use of the Bible is often depressingly functionalist – designed to extract information or direction; to serve some project or answer some doubt.

It is equally depressing that the many more modern people who are *not* churchgoers are – to a considerable degree – virtual 'outsiders' to the Bible. Our culture (in the UK at least) has not done all it could to maintain approach roads to it. The bits of it we continue to echo in our day to day speech may be broken fragments of what is little more than an 'asset-stripped' Bible. Like

Momo's ruined amphitheatre, it sits neglected on the outskirts of most people's day-to-day lives; few visit it, and some do not know that it is there at all.

How might habits of contemplative abiding help modern people to do what earlier users of the Bible once did – who knew instinctively how to find their way around the Bible, and in their theological imaginations to 'roam freely through the Sacred Writ'?[4] How might they be helped to emulate Momo, who doesn't arrive at the ruined amphitheatre either as an archaeologist or as a tourist, but comes to make it her home?

One very direct and obvious way in which a better capacity to dwell in the Bible could (and, in my view, should) be addressed – in the UK at any rate – is to make it far more central to the school curriculum than it presently is. I do not think that this needs to be at the expense of the sacred texts of other religious traditions, as will become plain. RE teaching tends to circle around questions of ethics, the philosophy of religion, and the study of ritual to the detriment of a thorough consideration of the religious texts that have played a foundational role in the shaping of human civilization. This is a serious loss to the religious literacy of future generations. If more time were taken to introduce the Bible to school-children in this country – nationwide – then it would take only a generation to restore to our nation an extraordinary power to imagine and describe with the help of this great resource.

I have remained grateful all my life to the teacher in my primary school who took us all the way through the stories of the patriarchs, from Genesis to Joshua, and who often dramatized his telling of them in the most vivid way so that we forgot the classroom altogether, and were – for example – suddenly *with* Moses in the desert. He let us colour in and decorate our exercise books, which made them quite unlike all our other books, and gave us licence to imagine the biblical world we were being encouraged to explore through our pictures and re-tellings. He gave me a feeling of being 'within' the Bible.

But, as I have already hinted, the problem is not only how to open up the Bible to the biblically-illiterate. It is also how to wean those who feel themselves to be on good terms with the Bible from the view that they have it all taped.

This is because the idea that one is on top of something, and has mastery of it, can itself precisely have a *distancing* effect. The object of one's supposed knowledge loses its power to surprise and transform; the moment it becomes commonplace, it becomes an instrument in our hands that we can pick up and put down at will. When we have used it for whatever purpose we wanted it for, we can hang it up in its regular place and walk off.

Paradoxically, then – for those who have some knowledge of the Bible already – the intensification process may need to begin with something that in one way or another makes the Bible more strange than it was before. Something valuable and liberating can happen when in encountering the Bible someone who supposed she knew what she was dealing with suddenly finds it a bit less familiar than it was. But (and this is the paradox) oddity can lead to intimacy. Through moments of de-familiarization, a better abiding can emerge. This is because one achieves a greater presence to an object or another person (a presence more like Momo's) when one has set aside one's preconceptions about them. One can be led to look harder by realizing the sheer otherness of something

– the fact that it is not just an extension of oneself, one's wishes and purposes. One can be sent back to it with new energy and interest

So, as promised, in what follows, I am going to make three suggestions for ways in which that feeling of contemplative abiding with Scripture (perhaps even of abiding *in* Scripture) might be fostered in its readers today, aiming to deliver biblically over-familiar people (as much as biblically estranged ones) into a new intimacy with these extraordinary texts.

The various suggestions I will make for how modern people might better abide with the Bible are quite diverse, and not all of them will be to everyone's taste, or within everyone's realm of possibility. They are not anything so organized as a scheme or programme. But what they do all have in common is a desire to disrupt commonplace, instrumentalizing uses of the Bible – to make Scripture *strange* – so as to intensify our presence to it, and its presence to us.

1 Read Slowly, and as Though in the Presence of a 'You'

Momo will be a help in two ways here, and the first is by her example. In approaching the

Bible, it's possible to learn something valuable by imagining oneself *as* Momo – or at least as an imitator of her gift of listening.

Momo has attentiveness and sympathy, and above all she has *time*. 'Some things need time', says the narrator, 'and time was the one thing in which Momo was rich'. Indeed, the book as a whole is a story about time and our need of it. Her contemplation was never hurried. The reading of the Bible in a spirit of devotion should never be hurried either. If time *is* limited, it is better to read less of the Bible slowly than more of it quickly.

There are particular analogies to be drawn here with the ancient Christian tradition of *lectio divina*. I referred to it indirectly earlier in the chapter; it's that slow, contemplative praying of Scripture which remains alive in the monastic, and especially the Benedictine, tradition. In a way that recalls the rabbinic injunction to 'turn, and turn it again' (referring to the Torah),[5] *lectio divina* involves reading and re-reading a single passage of the Bible in the expectation that new levels of meaning will open up each time. The text will be internalized – *ingested* and *digested* in a way that is often compared explicitly with eucharistic participation. In a way that closely parallels the sacrament, this way of relating to Scripture *unites the believer to God*, and Scripture (like the sacrament) is seen by the practitioners of *lectio divina* as given by God for just this purpose.

Thus, in a manner that stands in stark opposition to our contemporary culture's habits of speed reading, the practice of *lectio divina* will begin with us 'taking in the word' (a model here is provided by Mary, 'treasuring all these things in her heart' (Luke 2.19) – letting the mysteries of God's purpose abide *in her* as well as abiding *with them* by pondering them). The text we choose to ponder may be a verse or a portion of a verse – even just a word or two. We should gently repeat it (*meditatio*), allowing it 'to interact with our thoughts, our hopes, our memories [and] our desires',[6] the whole process leading eventually to prayer (*oratio*), as loving dialogue with God and consecration of our will to him, and to contemplation (*contemplatio*), as delighted rest in God's presence. In this way, the same simple text can elicit responses from its readers at multiple levels.

The dialogue that can open up in the slow reading which is *lectio divina* is a valuable reminder that we are not alone when we read it; we are in the presence of God.

In Spring 2010, the performance artist Marina Abramović presented a work entitled *The Artist is Present* to the public. She sat in the Museum of Modern Art in New York City, at a table with an empty chair opposite her in which visitors to the museum were invited to sit for as long as they wanted to.

She sat there all the time that the museum was open to the public, from before it opened each day until after it had closed, for a period of nearly three months. It was a total of around 700 hours of contemplating (and being contemplated by) the succession of people that came and shared her table. Their faces were documented by a photographer (along with a note of how long each of them sat in the chair), and can be viewed online as part of the record of this performance.[7] One of the most extraordinary things about the photographs is that they show very different responses being drawn from the different visitors: there are a number of photographs that show the people sitting with Abramović to have been weeping, for example.

MoMA send us back to Momo, for (as I said at the beginning of this section) there are two ways in which Momo might illuminate what it means to relate contemplatively to the Bible. The first was by her listening example. But she also functions in the book, at times, a little bit *like* the Bible, and especially like the parts of it we might initially find inscrutable. Marina Abramović seemed to function in something of the same way, for some of her visitors.

Here is an example from Michael Ende's story. Two men from the town who have borne a violent grudge against one another for ages come into the presence of Momo, and their uncertain speculations about what she might be thinking led them through a series of outbursts, rhetorical questions, confessions, and eventually a rapprochement with each other. They do not get advice from her, but somehow the space she gives them to articulate whatever is in their minds helps them to come to a new point of view.

The Bible is perhaps not best described as a silent listener to us, like some sort of non-directive counsellor, but it *can* at times resist our desire to get immediate advice or guidance from it. And it can *very definitely* resist our desire to make it confirm our pre-conceived points of view. This can be very good for us, but it will only happen if we stay in its presence long enough to ask the question whether our points of view really *are* pre-conceived (as the two arguing men stayed in Momo's presence until they questioned their certainties about one another).

The Bible is not just a tool. It is a 'You', not an 'It'. To open it is to come into the presence of something living and transformative; something actively present. To abide with it is to recognize, moreover, that it is what the contemporary French Catholic philosopher Jean-Luc Marion might call a 'saturated phenomenon', one that contains more than any one reader or any one epoch can simply and completely and definitively wring out of it. Its power to affect successive new situations and to encounter new people is apparently limitless. It is a text that keeps on giving.

The saturated nature of the Bible can have the effect of a sort of 'bedazzlement',[8] which is itself transformative. John Bunyan, whose *Pilgrim's Progress* 'seems like a journey through Scripture itself',[9] is a consummate historical example of someone who finds the Bible to be 'bedazzling' in this way. Often, his relationship with the Bible is a turbulent one, in which he can be hurled into despair, or can find different biblical passages fighting with one another in his mind like Jacob and Esau. At other and happier times, as Bunyan writes, Scriptures are 'made to spangle in mine eyes'; and, he goes on, 'I have sometimes seen more in a line of the Bible than I could well tell how to stand under...'[10]

A willingness to receive from the Bible is best nurtured when one is respectful of its resistance to being rendered into some neat 'conclusion' or 'message'. You can look at photographs of Marina Abramović's artwork *The Artist is Present*, or read descriptions of it, but they will never substitute for the live performance itself – the infinite depth that opens up when two people face one another in real time. Likewise, there is no substitute for living encounter with the Bible itself; it cannot be replaced with a set of bullet points. It is too saturated for that.

2 Read With Strange Others
In this section I want to suggest we have a lot to gain from reading the Bible in the company

of 'strange others', who will alert us to things in the texts that we might otherwise miss. Some of these strange others will be Christians who, like Bunyan, come from earlier epochs. Some will be from outside the Christian tradition altogether.

Reading in the company of historical figures might sound like an arcane, or perhaps just boring suggestion, but it can be a very extraordinary thing to discover what earlier Christians, with whom present day ones share the communion of saints, made of Scriptural passages that we think we understand perfectly well – passages whose meanings we think are quite 'obvious'. We may not agree with the interpretations of earlier readers of Scripture (many of them will remain permanently bizarre or whimsical to us), but this doesn't mean we should not be instructed by those readers' sense of bedazzlement at Scripture, and what emerged from their own particular attempts to abide with it.

Jewish midrashic tradition reproduces the Hebrew text of the Torah with wide margins around it full of what that tradition has determined to be the most authoritative or illuminating interpretations of it over the centuries (and the fact that these interpretations do not all agree with one another is something that is prized because of the ongoing stimulus of such disagreements for later readers). The Scriptural text's dialogue with the history of its interpretation has always kept the original text lively for Jewish readers. Some medieval Christians had an equivalent to this in the so-called *glossa ordinaria*, in which classic commentary from the Church Fathers was reproduced along with the canonical text. But modern Christians are generally not fortunate enough to have Bibles reproduced in this way. In an age in which weblinks and hypertext are ever more familiar parts of our practices of reading, perhaps we are in a position once again to make more of our histories of interpretation. They could help us to abide more, not less, searchingly with the Bible itself.

If we are likely to find it startling to come across medieval monks devoting hundreds of pages to their interpretations of the erotic passages of the Song of Songs, or early Church Fathers seeing Christ in every narrative detail of the Pentateuch, then we may find ourselves equally surprised by what some of our living contemporaries make of the Christian Bible, when they approach it from the perspective of another religious tradition. But this too can be an extraordinarily productive experience for Christian readers.

The novelist Walker Percy contrasts the experience of the first European ever to see the Grand Canyon with that of the modern sightseer. The modern sightseer will find it almost impossible to really look at the canyon. This is because:

> the Grand Canyon, the thing as it is,
> has been appropriated by the symbolic
> complex which has already been formed
> in the sightseer's mind [...] The thing
> is no longer the thing as it confronted
> the Spaniard; it is rather that which has
> already been formulated – by picture
> postcard, geography book, tourist folders,
> and the words *Grand Canyon*. As a
> result of this preformulation, the source
> of the sightseer's pleasure undergoes a
> shift. Where the wonder and delight of
> the Spaniard arose from his penetration
> of the thing itself, from a progressive
> discovery of depths, patterns, colors,
> shadows, etc., now the sightseer measures
> his satisfaction *by the degree to which*

> *the canyon conforms to the preformed complex.*[11]

For the past 15 years or so I have been involved in a very unusual experiment in the study of sacred texts which has academic beginnings but is now rooted as a practice in grass-roots communities in London and other cities around the world. It is a practice of co-reading Scriptural texts from the three so-called 'Abrahamic' traditions – Judaism, Islam and Christianity – by small groups of devoted practitioners of those three faiths, and its name is Scriptural Reasoning (SR). SR disrupts in a healthy way the habits of reading that Christian people can allow themselves to get into – stale oppositions between 'liberal' and 'conservative' readings; over-doctrinalized readings; readings that in one way or another take the text too much for granted.

To build on Walker Percy's example, it introduces people who think they know what the Bible says ('what the Grand Canyon *should* look like') to people who are seeing it for the first time. The introduction of an 'other' (or more than one 'other') to the activity of studying Scripture within a particular tradition can have radical and helpful effects, many of which are precisely a deepening of the relation of a particular tradition's Scripture readers to their own Scriptures, without this implying any kind of syncretism or watering down of commitment or devotion in the name of a multi-faith synthesis.

My experience as a Christian is that reading the Christian Bible with Jews and Muslims is reading that will potentially be interrupted and illuminated in new ways. These others are invited to co-read, to ask questions and become contributors to the process of suggesting possible answers to the questions – and one of the common consequences of this is that the texts open up unexpected meanings for me (whose sacred texts the Christian Scriptures *are*) even at the same time as participants from the other Abrahamic traditions learn more about a text that is *not* theirs. Something analogous happens, but in reverse, when the Qur'an or Hebrew Bible are read and Christians comment on it to their Muslim and Jewish co-readers.

One of the obvious effects of putting members of different faiths in front of the texts of traditions that are not their own is that they want to know what these texts *mean*, and how they are made sense of by those whose texts they are. This is good. A person whose texts are being studied at any particular point *ought* to be adopting an interrogative attitude towards them in the same way as a visitor to the Grand Canyon ought to be trying to look beyond her 'preformed complex'. Often the questions of the other religionists can help her to do this, as she will not always have an answer to their questions, and this will get her questioning hard herself.

These moments of losing one's hold on the text are very common in SR, and they are often described as moments when the text seems to 'collapse' or to 'explode'. In a session that is working well, this can be the beginning of an extremely creative re-engagement with the text, and with a partici-pant's own identity in relation to the God whom she believes has given her the text and wants her to wrestle with it. There can be a vigorous time of proposing solutions to the problems the text has thrown up – or ways of reconstructing it after it has apparently collapsed or exploded. Co-readers from the other traditions are often surprisingly helpful in the reconstruction process.

Part of their profound gift to the process is their offering of the readings that propose themselves as most natural to *them*, some of which may be quite new and quite exciting to the reader who is over-familiar with established ways of looking at the text. And of course – to reiterate – the process is constantly working in all directions; it is not only a question of Christians receiving useful new perspectives from Jews and Muslims. Christians will interrogate the texts (and readers) of Judaism and Islam, and find themselves made constructive in the interpretative activity of those other traditions. They will learn a great deal about those texts in the process.

Not every Christian has willing Jews or Muslims in their neighbourhood with whom to read. But I wonder whether some of the same results might come from reading with people who have no particular religious commitment at all. There are many people who respond with interest to the idea of getting to know the contents of the world's biggest best-seller, a book that has so profoundly shaped the world we inhabit. They will certainly bring their own stimulating questions to the reading of it.

3 Read With the Help of the Arts

Finally, I want to think about the contemplation of the Bible in relation to art. And first, here, I want to explore how contemporary Christians might relate to the Bible in a way that is *analogous* with the way they might relate to art.

The art critic Roger Fry, writing in 1919, discussed two kinds of seeing – or, rather, as he put it, the difference between *seeing* and *looking*. Seeing is a useful skill that nature has given us. It has to do with the use that appearances have for the business of living. In other words it is functional. We extract key information as rapidly as possible from this kind of seeing. It tells whether the movement in the long grass is the wind or a tiger about to pounce; whether the Gucci handbag is real or a fake; and whether the bread has gone mouldy.

Looking, on the other hand, seems less obviously to have any utility value. It is what appreciative viewers of art do, and the non-utilitarian character of such looking leads Fry to say that 'biologically speaking, art is a blasphemy'.[12] Why might the making and sharing of art be an offence against biology? For Fry (who delights in the offence!) it is because it serves no obvious purpose. Looking, writes Fry, is a type of vision that is 'quite distinct from the practical vision of our instinctive life'. When we *look*, our vision 'dwells much more consciously and deliberately' upon the object in front of us. Fry thinks children have a special capacity for this, because they have not yet fully learnt the more defensive techniques of mere 'seeing'. They look at things, he says, with '*passion*'. We might say that Fry's model of looking is a mode of *abiding*.

I am not qualified to comment on how good Fry is as an evolutionary biologist, but I still find the contrast he draws a meaningful one. It reminds me of the story of Moses' encounter with the Burning Bush in the Book of Exodus, and the very odd fact that we are told *twice* that Moses looks at the bush. The passage goes like this:

> Moses *looked*, and the bush was blazing,
> yet it was not consumed. Then Moses
> said, 'I must turn aside and *look at* this
> great sight, and see why the bush is not
> burned up.' (Exodus 3.2-3; my emphasis)

First he simply sees it, and computes it as a peculiar physical fact. But then he *goes over and looks* at it – a second looking which has involved him in turning aside from his intended path. It has led him to stop, turn, and really look. It becomes a moment not just for the extraction of information. Once he has turned aside to look, the voice of God in the Burning Bush can really address him. Moses takes his sandals off, prostrates himself, and is transformed. This is now a moment of relationship.

Christians of many traditions have looked at visual art – *really* looked, in the second sense of looking – for centuries. They have done so in the context of worship, such that the art became a part of their worship. Visual art in churches often had a liturgical role, and in adorning the great sacramental actions of the Church (like the eucharist and baptism), it showed an affinity with those sacraments. In a certain extended sense, it became sacramental itself.

Altarpieces are a good example. They are made to attend the sacrament of the eucharist (itself compared in Christian tradition with the Burning Bush), and as the ordinary natural objects of bread and wine are 'enflamed' by the Spirit, it can sometimes seem as though the paintings that surround the eucharistic action, with their own natural materials of wood, and paint and gold leaf, are kindled too – drawing the sustained gaze of those who, like Moses, are ready to turn aside and abide with them. Altarpieces were designed to draw Christian people to deeper contemplation of the mystery of the eucharist that was celebrated on the holy table.

They ask to be contemplated, to be looked at with passion, as Moses gazed at the Burning Bush. And many of the viewers of these paintings who have over the centuries adopted that sort of looking, have – like Moses – found themselves addressed as they look.

Art for liturgical spaces is an art made to serve not only contemplation but devotion; to make its viewers aware that they are on holy ground, in the presence of the Living God. The disclosure of God in them is not, of course, commanded by the artist's skill, any more than it is by the human performance of set liturgical actions; it remains wholly God's initiative, wholly a matter of grace. But God is a God who is generous in making himself known in the context of worship, and who bestows himself through its material forms.

67

The interpretation of Scripture should have the same quality of enraptured contemplation that such artists both model and inspire. It can be devotional interpretation of a sort that many religious painters were engaged in *themselves*, and that their works aimed to encourage in *others*. The arts (not just painting, of course, but poetry, drama, music, architecture, dance) can in this way re-educate the modern reader of the Bible to read more richly – more traditionally but simultaneously more creatively – than they would otherwise do. They bequeath to us some wonderful exercises in contemplative dwelling in the Bible: inspiring models – every bit as inspiring as my RE teacher was 35 years ago, and available to many more people.

One of my favourite poets is Henry Vaughan (1621–95). Vaughan's poems, written out of an acute sense of exile, were composed in the time of Cromwell's Protectorate, in a valley near the one I grew up in: the Usk. He described wandering in landscapes that, when I first read him, I recognized as my own. His church – the episcopally-led Church of England which would be re-established at the time of the Restoration – had had its forms of worship suppressed. And so, denied his liturgies and his sacraments, Vaughan was forced to look for grace elsewhere, in a very English (or in this case, Anglo-Welsh) combination of (i) Scripture, which *was* still available to him, and (ii) observation of the natural world.

The Bible – in the King James Version – often tops or tails his poems. These verses from the Book of Acts conclude his characteristically longing poem *The Search*:

Acts xvii 27-28

That they should seek the Lord, if haply they might feel after him, and find him, though he be not far off from every one of us, for in him we live, and move, and have our being.

After a journey through a series of biblical locations, Vaughan's inner promptings take him off to the wilderness, where Christ both faced temptation and found retreat. Here the ascended Christ still feels near to Vaughan. And this, Vaughan surmises, is the place the true Church (*his* church, not Cromwell's) now finds her destiny lying. It is hard not to hear his descriptions of this desert space as descriptions of the Welsh valleys:

> What silent paths, what shades, and cells,
> Fair, virgin-flowers, and hallowed *wells...*

But, of course, that is precisely the aim of these extraordinary flights of biblical and poetic imagination; they are to make sense of his environment – however unpromising it may seem; however far from grace – as a place of revelation and divine touch. Vaughan has a heightened awareness that Christ sat on the ground, drank from springs, and wandered the earth's paths, just as he does now. In a powerfully beautiful phrase, used of the peregrinations of the seraphim with whom Jesus shared the wilderness, Vaughan says that Jesus 'heavened their *walks*'.[13] The desert is sanctified, and the 'wild shades' are made a paradise by Jesus's presence there. The aptness of the verses from Acts is apparent – 'he be not far off from every one of us, for in him we live, and move, and have our being'. That vision awoke in me, as a teenager, a sense that what might initially seem lonely places, out of the way, neglected, forgotten, are places where miracles might happen.

Vaughan could let the world that the Bible described and imagined infuse the way he viewed and experienced his own rural landscape, so that whenever he looked at a grove of trees or a river he saw angels talking with patriarchs (Abraham discoursing and eating, Jacob wrestling, and Elijah being fed). To use his own language, he let the Bible 'heaven' his landscape, and this relatively unforced imposition of a Scriptural template upon the landscape he lived in, to create a Scriptural-natural palimpsest, is an extraordinary achievement.

Vaughan gives us a magnificent example of how literature in particular has been an exercise in contemplative dwelling in the Bible. His contemplative vision can be not only shared but imitated (as Momo's can be imitated). But this requires both a deep familiar knowledge of the Bible that can only be the product of regular exposure to it, and also a readiness to *imagine with it* – to imagine the world in its terms. What the arts have above all to teach modern readers of the Bible is the power and possibilities of the human imagination when faced with a text. Imaginative activity is a sort of dwelling-within a narrative, a vision, or some other poetic world. It is therefore in its unique way a sort of abiding.

Coda

Paul writes to the Romans in an epistle set for the First Sunday in Lent that 'the word is near you, on your lips and in your heart' (Romans 10.8b). In London's National Gallery there is a painting that is all about receiving the Word into the deepest intimacy with oneself: Fra Filippo Lippi's *Annunciation*, painted sometime between 1450 and 1453.[14] It is a painting about contemplation as the means to union with God. Mary herself is often compared to the Burning Bush – enkindled but not consumed by God's presence within her. But here she is also in the position of Moses – the one who moves from 'biological' or functionalist seeing to the absorbed looking of the heart.

Unlike many images of the annunciation in which the Holy Spirit – as a dove or a ray of light – approaches Mary's ear, here the dove approaches her belly, with which it is absolutely level. And the seed of God's unexpected and surprising Word is emitted as a stream of golden light from the dove's beak, and bursts in a little splash of answering light where there is a small parting in her tunic. It has been pointed out that Mary's womb, receiving God's light through this aperture, is like an eye – and, indeed, the fifteenth century science of the eye called the membranes of the eye around the opening of the pupil its 'tunic'.[15]

Lippi is suggesting to us that Mary's womb has become an eye; it's as if her whole *being* has become a *looking*, and she is full of God's light. This looking leads to conception, for through the eye of Mary's womb the Light of the World takes bodily shape within her.

A Lenten aspiration might be to make our *eyes* like Mary's *womb*, both when they read the Bible but also in other moments of looking, as when we (like Henry Vaughan) survey our surroundings, and realize that our world is the same world that the Bible describes; the world where God moves. We can ask that through faithful and open looking a sort of conception may happen within us as a sort of conception happened in Mary – an emotional, imaginative and intellectual conception, in this case; a conception of the great truth about God which great Christian art serves, and which the Scriptures invite us to receive.

3
ABIDING THROUGH CARE

B rave Sir Robin is a character in *Monty Python and the Holy Grail*, one of a series of knights who go off to try to find the grail, each meeting with one or another kind of failure. Robin's problems are twofold. First, he is actually rather cowardly; and second, he is afflicted by a minstrel who follows him everywhere singing about all the awful things that might be about to happen to him, but which (the minstrel thinks) he will be far too brave to mind about:

> He was not in the least bit scared to be
> mashed into a pulp
> Or to have his eyes gouged out and his
> elbows broken,
> To have his kneecaps split and his body
> burned away
> And his limbs all hacked and mangled,
> brave Sir Robin.

Eventually, 'brave' Sir Robin's nerve is completely shattered, and at the first sign of trouble he gives the entire quest up. But, humiliatingly, the minstrel goes on singing:

> Brave Sir Robin ran away
> Bravely ran away, away...
> When danger reared its ugly head
> He bravely turned his tail and fled,
> Yes, brave Sir Robin turned about
> And gallantly he chickened out,
> Bravest of the brave, Sir Robin.

Sir Robin is the victim of a belief that courage in the face of deadly dangers is the only honourable form of abiding. This is what the minstrel constantly reinforces in him, like some paralysing inner voice. The only way to abide well is to seek out enemies and face them down. The quintessential abider will be armour-clad and strong.

This chapter is a denial of that false belief (a belief that is Sir Robin's undoing, because he simply cannot live up to it). Or at any rate, this chapter is prepared to countenance the idea that there may be more than one sort of bravery, and that not all bravery is about derring-do. This chapter is about *care*, and care as something closely related to *presence*. As I will argue towards the close of the chapter, being genuinely present to someone who is in need of care is often itself a brave activity – it just won't be armour-clad. Caring requires that the carer should not – like Brave Sir Robin – run away. But it also suggests that, in some way, running away has already begun from the first moment that armour is ever donned. Gung-ho ethics of courage are themselves – quite often – a sort of flight. Caring demands a different sort of courage.

Even when his or her practical resources are very few, in terms of weapons or skills for combatting a challenge or solving a problem, each person faced with another in need still has room to care, and the resource that remains to her is the resource of staying present. To recall again Rowan Williams's newspaper article on Christmas Eve 2011, care can be expressed in transformative ways by the mere act of being there – of not going away. This is especially true '[w]hen people are pushed by all sorts of destructive forces into seeing themselves as hopeless, as rubbish, so that what they do doesn't matter any more':

> 'I'm not going away' is one of the most important things we can ever hear,

whether we hear it from someone at our
bedside in illness or over a shared drink
at a time of depression or stress – or
at a moment when we wonder what's
happening to our neighbourhood and
our society.

I'm reminded by these words of the typology developed by Sam Wells, now Vicar of St Martin in the Fields in London, a church whose famous 'ever open door' has made it a place that very successfully communicates its 'being there' in the heart of London. I have adapted it slightly in what follows, but the key points are the same.[1]

There are ways, says Wells, in which God in Jesus Christ (i) *works with*, and (ii) *works for* his beloved people.

Jesus's active three years of ministry, in which he calls and trains his disciples to continue his work in the power of the Spirit after he has gone, can be understood as God, in Christ, *working with* his people: bringing them along with him as he teaches and getting them to help him in his mission.

Jesus's Passion, from the moment of his arrest in Gethsemane until his entry into death with that great, loud cry, can be seen as God, in Christ, *working for* his people. Jesus must fulfil this part of his ministry alone. No one can share this part of the journey with him, and where he is going we cannot come. This is what traditional doctrines of the atonement have explored as its 'substitutionary' aspect: Jesus takes our place; he is for us in a work that we cannot accomplish on our own behalf.

But Wells highlights another way in which God is in Christ – not the three years of active ministry, nor the week of lonely suffering, but the *thirty* years before Jesus's public ministry has begun; this period of time Wells calls 'Nazareth'. Much less is said about it in the New Testament than about the period of time that follows it, but without that time Jesus's *working with* and *working for* could not have happened. It is his *being with* his people. Such *being with* is the consequence of the incarnation, of Jesus's being born into a human family, learning language, growing up, learning a trade, being part of a worshipping community, eating, drinking, sleeping.

It is different from the other two ways in which God is, because it is not goal-oriented in the same way. It is a simple but amazing fact, a miraculously 'natural' solidarity with human life, an abiding in and through the day to day. It has some of the qualities of what in this chapter I will argue that 'care' should manifest, in its simple alongsideness. The messianic name 'Emmanuel' – God-with-us – pays tribute to this aspect of God's care for us. Our calling to care takes its cue from this initiative on God's part.

In what follows, I want to suggest four models of care that I regard as important and valuable in Christian terms, especially when taken together. The first three all have elements in them of *working with* or *working for*. The final one is care as simply *being with*. Indeed, the final model is a suggestion that this being with – this *abiding* – is a uniquely pure and necessary form of care. All the other kinds would mean a great deal less if they did not have it in view.

The model for whatever sorts of caring are 'godly' will, for Christians, be drawn from Jesus's own example and teaching. They will also be rooted in Christian practices of worship, which is itself better described as a being with than as any sort of working for. Worship is being with God, and being with each other in being with God. It is true that the root meaning of the Greek word 'liturgy' is work, but – in a move reminiscent of Jesus's parables – the familiar idea of work has been turned on its head when it turns into worship. Worship is the *Lord's* work – the work of the Kingdom – and at its centre are disciplines that require us to acknowledge our dependency and limits, and set other values alongside our prizing of efficiency, utility, and power. As Rowan Williams puts it in a discussion specifically of inter-cession: 'intercession acknowledges the reality of the need of others and one's own powerlessness in respect of their future'.[2] Unsurprisingly, the mechanized modern culture they live in makes Western people think in management categories a great deal of the time; most human activities are now measured by the processes rather than the relationships that constitute those activities. In Wells's words:

> it's possible to be the recipient of a
> person's help and still find the benefactor
> remains a stranger to you. The whole
> point of the professional infrastructure

81

of divided offices, administrative
assistants, appointment times and special
uniforms is to remind all parties that
this isn't a friendship, with expectations
of compassion and tenderness, but the
provision of a service with no strings
attached outside and beyond that
service.[3]

The *working for* model, and some versions of the
working with model, are prone to turn everything
into 'a problem ripe for solving'. But, as Wells
says, 'some things aren't problems, and some
problems can't simply be fixed'.[4]

So here are four aspects of a Christian ethic of care,
for which (by contrast with the courage asked of
Brave Sir Robin) the key courage required is
mainly the courage to stay present.

1 Arguing

Arguing is closely related to prophecy. To argue
with someone is to take the trouble to remain
with them, in dialogue and sometimes in struggle.
It is therefore much more obviously a form
of care than simply disengaging from them or
abandoning them. Walking away is sometimes

held up as a model of tolerant good practice in our contemporary society – leaving other people with their opinions while I hold tightly on to mine. It is a terrible model. I do not want to claim that all arguing is good – it can be brutal, one-sided, obsessive, and desirous less of the good of the other than of the other's being beaten down and rendered voiceless. But the loss of good-quality argument as a mode of care is a cause of the often-remarked-upon attenuation of a deliberative ideal in our public and private reasonings.[5]

Jesus argues a great deal of the time, and so do the prophets (and so does Paul). It is quite cognate with actions we more naturally associate with a liturgically-learnt Christian pattern of life – actions like praise and thanksgiving, confession, petitioning, and blessing. All of these encode profound truths about what makes the world the way it is and how it can most fully order itself to express that reality.

Good liturgical actions correspond to something about what we might tentatively call the world's 'operating conditions' in God. The performance of them is therefore, we might say, a way of making the world *more real*, by helping it to enact and display its profoundest truths. Human beings are transformed, and *themselves* become *more real*, by their participation in the Church's liturgies. And if, as I believe, one of the human transformations most importantly and profoundly generated by good liturgy is what might be called greater belonging in *the world as it should be*, then one of the practical effects of that will be a dissatisfaction with the *world as it is*, and this may lead to argumentative encounters. For it is important to emphasize that Christian belonging in the world is not the same thing as *conformity* to the world. It could be described as a sort of 'excess of belonging' (or, perhaps, an 'excess of care'). This sort of 'excessive belonging' may take the form of more exalted joy, of heightened responsibility, or precisely of sharper prophetic critique. It can issue in critical challenges and high expectations.

Liturgy – at its best – trains Christians not only to confess, petition, bless and so on, but also to interrogate the world, imagine alternative ways things could be, and advance arguments for such alternatives, precisely as a mode of care. One can care, just as one can belong, by arguing. Prophetic argument is after all a way of telling the

world that it does not yet belong to itself suffi-
ciently well; that it is falling short. Who would
bother to do this if they didn't care?

2 Healing and Forgiving Sins

Therapeutic care is – for very obvious reasons – a
paradigmatic case of what care is, for Christians
and non-Christians alike. But Christians find
themselves under an obligation to consider the
meaning of therapeutic care in constant relation
to the forgiveness of sins, which is pronounced
regularly in the context of liturgical worship,
and which is also – frequently and influentially
– explored in Christian tradition through the
metaphor of healing.

For St Augustine of Hippo, a lead image for the
operation of grace is that of medicine, and for
Christ is that of the physician. Augustine interprets the parable of the Good Samaritan, in a
tour de force of allegorical reading, as the whole
of salvation history in miniature, with the central
motif – the central saving act – being the healing
of the man half dead by the side of the road.[6]
Augustine's arguments with the Pelagians (and
their less extreme cousins the 'Semi-Pelagians')[7]
circle repeatedly around the human condition as

one of deep woundedness. The Pelagians thought human wills were still in good enough shape after the Fall to make them capable of choosing to act without sin. Augustine thought that God's forgiveness (and not some superhuman ability to be one's own doctor) was the only solution to the injury that sin had inflicted. Grace, in other words, was to be understood as a form of *care*.[8]

And if that is the case, then it is possible and proper to regard human care as a participation in God's work of grace. But the discipline here, at each point, is not to allow care of the body to become artificially separated from tending to the needs of a wounded soul (for what God has joined together, human beings should not put asunder.)

The tradition of palliative care in hospices has provided a context in which this insight can be powerfully and movingly explored. When your patients are all terminally ill, the objectives of therapeutic care have to shift; if the point of the care is not repair of a bodily system then other aspects of care come much more centrally into view, and especially the emotional, psychological and spiritual needs of the person who is dying. This will often include a concern for creating the circumstances in which a dying person can be reconciled with events or people from her past, if at all possible. This may involve chaplains, counsellors and family members as well as doctors and nurses. Healing the wounds of sin takes place alongside a very intensive care for the (dying) body.

The hospice movement, and those involved in hospital chaplaincy, need every support from Christians as they seek to ensure that emotional, psychological and spiritual concerns are taken more seriously in *all* aspects of medical care and not only at the end of life.

The word 'Paraclete' is a hugely suggestive word in the context of this sort of care. It is a word that is first used of God (the Spirit) in God's activity of healing, defending, comforting, and so on, but might also be appropriately used of human carers. As Jean Vanier helpfully points out, '[e]tymologically, the word "paraclete" means "the one who answers the call"':

> What a beautiful name!
> God is the one who answers the cry of
> the weak and those in need.

A mother is a 'paraclete' for her child
when she answers the cry of her little
one,
holds and loves him or her.
Every time we look after a person in need
and answer their cry,
we become paracletes.
Jesus was a paraclete for his disciples.[9]

Caring of this kind is a sharing in the divine compassion. And in passing, we could remark here that because the origins of *law*, too, at least in Hebrew tradition, are fundamentally about how to address cries, then law too can be understood as an attempt to act therapeutically. Much of the law in the Old Testament is accompanied by the warning that if victims have no functioning law to protect them, their cries will be heard by God, and this will be to the judgement of the people who let them get into that parlous state:

You shall not abuse any widow or
orphan. If you do abuse them, when they
cry out to me, I will surely heed their cry
[…].
    If you lend money to my people, to
the poor among you, you shall not deal

with them as a creditor; you shall not
exact interest from them. If you take
your neighbour's cloak in pawn, you shall
restore it before the sun goes down; for it
may be your neighbour's only clothing to
use as cover; in what else shall that person
sleep? And if your neighbour cries out to
me, I will listen, for I am compassionate.
(Exodus 22.22-27)

Law is concerned to repair social arrangements
in which there are cries – to respond in the
mode of a 'paraclete'. But it is also concerned,
where it can, to *pre-empt* the situations which
generate such cries in the first place. In both
respects, law itself can be considered a mode
of care.

3 Hosting

A consideration of hosting as a mode of care
makes it necessary to think again – as in Chapter
1 – about space and how it is tended and put to
use. It is a particularly important category for an
established Church, like the Church of England
to which I belong, as it thinks about its human
responsibilities for the cure of souls in relation to
physical geography.

Place is not just constituted by geographical features like rivers, mountain ranges, desert, oceans and so on. It is constituted by people and their relationships. Hostile relationships tend to result in the demarcation of formal (quantitative) 'spaces', whose patrolled boundaries are shown as lines on maps. Caring relationships tend to result in the emergence of (qualitative) *places*, which accumulate associations and meanings for people, and in which they associate.[10]

In endorsing this insight, I would want to give my own example of relationally-constituted space in action – on a relatively small scale but not, I think, an inconsequential one. As part of my work with the Cambridge Inter-Faith Programme I was involved in developing the idea of a 'Tent' adjacent to the St Ethelburga's Centre for Reconciliation and Peace in London. It was opened in 2004. It is a real tent of the sort you might find in a Middle Eastern desert, and it sits there behind the church building on Bishopsgate, where there had for more than ten years been only a piece of waste ground left by the IRA bomb that went off nearby in 1993. It is now used as a place of meeting for those interested in furthering the dialogue between religious traditions and communities.

Leaving to one side any kitsch elements of the physical space of the tent, one can nonetheless endorse its signalling (by its physical provisionality – a tent being a temporary and mobile structure) of the fact that the *really important* space is that made in the relationships between the people who meet in it.

When it was opened, I found myself suddenly struck by the fact that the Prince of Wales, the Bishop of London, and the Lord Mayor were present in the tent. In their persons, they represented the ancient patterns of relationship between Crown, Church, and Civic or Municipal Authority which have *made* the public space which is London. Public space – or place – is not just lying there ready to be dropped in and out of. It has no neutral, ready-made character. It is always *mutual* ground, created by sets of relationships and commitments between institutions, traditions and the people who represent them. Facing the Prince, the Bishop and the Mayor in the Tent were a Christian, a Jew and a Muslim, who described the way they and their traditions had been coming into relationship in a new way through the reading of their Scriptures together – the practice of Scriptural Reasoning which I introduced in the previous chapter. And here too – represented in the bodies of three people – it was possible to see a new sort of public space being constituted that was relational and was not there before (by contrast with the fantasies of the advocates of religious pluralism who presuppose a common ground for inter-religious encounter that is simply there and ready for occupation).

They meet not only for their own interest or their own good, but with genuine concern (as religious people) for the good of their city – finding in their respective traditions reasons to *care* about that wider community of the non-religious as well as the religious in which they live. The patterns of relationship of Christianity, Judaism and Islam with each other – always embodied in actual collections of people – can make 'place' or destroy it.

The modern secular world's diminished conception of what makes public space may explain why it today seems so neglected and under threat – with few willing to take respon-sibility for it, to want to decorate it, love it, or volunteer to serve in it.

Public space needs care, and cannot be justified on the basis of a thin and generalized notion of 'tolerance'. In facing up to this, we will also need to face up to the fact that some people or communities will have both more reason and more resources to do the hosting. There is little point pretending otherwise in the name of some artificial egalitarian ideal. Anglicans could spend a lot of time apologizing for the inherited privileges they have, but it might be a better use of their energy to think more creatively about how to use those privileges for the benefit of those who live in the places they care for. And not all resources are those of property or power in any case. They may be resources of imagination and a sense of mutuality – which is why artists and Christian ministers may today find themselves in one another's company as they work for the regeneration of their communities.

Nonetheless, hosting – though validated by Jesus, who was both host and (even more often) guest – is in the end a 'working for' which, it will be no surprise, I think needs supplementation by my final category, which is care as simply 'being with'.

4 The Abiding That Is Simply 'Being With'

One of the key contrasts in John's Gospel is drawn by Jesus in a parable, and it's between the false shepherds, or hired hands, who run away, and the Good Shepherd, who *abides*.

The Good Shepherd stands as a contrast with Brave Sir Robin, with whom this chapter began, in two key ways, and the first is this simple fact that he does not run away. He will confront wolves if necessary. Meanwhile, Brave Sir Robin's similarity to the hired hands in Jesus's parable shows the shallowness of his commitment to the quest. A faithful knight, like a good shepherd, will be willing to lay down his life for the object of his concern, making his own self the guarantee of his faithfulness.

But the second contrast lies at an earlier stage, in the fact that a shepherd is not the same thing as a knight, and the abiding that is asked of each of them is not the same either. A knight is required to place himself *in extremis* – to seek out opportunities to confront, to oppose, and to endure. What this chapter has been arguing is that this is not the model of care that Jesus bequeaths to his followers. There is an abiding more profound, and more generous, in simple presence to one another.

In a previous section of this chapter, I discussed some of the special dimensions of therapeutic care that are practised in hospices. This was something I was privileged to witness and take part in when as a young adult I worked for some months as an auxiliary nurse in St Christopher's Hospice in Sydenham, South London – the pioneering hospice founded by Dame Cicely Saunders in 1967, and inspired by an explicitly Christian vision of care. Saunders insisted that the dying ask three things above all else: help me, listen to me, stay with me.

While there, I read Sheila Cassidy's extraordinary book *Sharing the Darkness*, which is itself all about hospice care, and is based on her own experience of running a hospice in the South West of England. One of the most memorable sections of that book is illustrated by a series of diagrams, in which a patient sits opposite a 'professional', who is kitted out with the uniform and tools of his or her profession. One is a doctor, with white coat and medical instruments. Another is a clergyman, with dog collar and prayer book.[11]

Cassidy points out the way in which these tools and outfits can be a form of self-protection – a carapace, something to hide behind, and (from the patient's point of view) a barrier that prevents her from receiving what she most needs. They can become like Sir Robin's armour and weaponry. This is not to say that uniforms and clearly defined roles do not sometimes have a helpful and reassuring part to play in human interaction. But they are best when they are a means to reaching someone ('getting over the threshold'[12]) rather than a means of maintaining an absolute boundary.

The challenge of caring for a dying person is that the effectiveness of the usual tools and roles is relativized. The patients are not going to get better, and they do not need a 'solution' to something. What will often be most precious to them, instead, is people who undertake to 'accompany' them in what they are going through. The final picture in the sequence has a naked person sitting in the 'professional's' chair.

The model of abiding that Jesus bequeaths to his disciples is not one in which the tick of the clock is accumulating units of expensive time, and the persons involved are either engaged in the targeted application of technical skill or professional know-how, but are attentively and mutually available to each other. They undertake 'accompaniment'.

I had two alcoholic parents. My father's alcoholism was apparent to us much earlier than my mother's. I remember becoming aware of it at around the age of 12, when we moved from a big Victorian school house in Durham, in the North East of England, in which my sister and I slept two storeys up from the ground floor, to our new home outside Chepstow on the Welsh borders, where the kitchen and dining room were just below our bedrooms. In the first house, we were insulated from the drinking and its effects. In the new house, assisted by our age and our later bedtimes as well as by the new domestic geography, we were exposed to pretty much every ugly feature of it. The incoherent, wounding circularity of my father's diatribes, the increasingly slurred speech, the furniture stumbled into and occasionally knocked over, and the eventual sound of his teetering (sometimes crawling on all fours) upstairs to bed. We would lie awake, holding our breath, until his bedroom door finally closed and the house fell silent.

My parents separated when I was a student and while my youngest sibling was still a teenager. My mother was in many ways a liberated person; she took A levels and went to university, graduating a few days before her sixtieth birthday. But her own drinking problems were becoming less and less easy to ignore. She lost energy and initiative, slept for a long time each afternoon, and by about halfway through the evening would often cease to be capable of a conversation that she could remember the following day. She became depressed, and the depression and the drinking formed a vicious circle.

The worst features of this strange life, for me, were – first – that each morning there was a pretence by all parties that our life was normal, that nothing out-of-the-ordinary had happened the previous evening; and – second – that all the time that my parents were together we very rarely had visitors to the house.

This second aspect of our life was in service of the first, as it meant that the only witnesses to the drinking were within the family. And so a new day would begin, and the pattern would repeat itself. I believe this will be a very familiar story to children who have grown up with alcoholic parents. I did in fact confront each of my parents about the fact that this unspoken truth of our family life was having destructive effects, and both – while sober – registered all the pain of it, and promised to do better. But sober alcoholics are different people from their drunk selves, and there is no continuity between the promises made by one and the actions performed by the other.

The reason I have gone into this piece of personal history is that I often think that the greatest damage an alcoholic does to his or her family is not to *be there*. My mother especially was someone we loved immensely when she was sober, and miss profoundly now that she is gone (she died in 2009). She was intelligent, funny and creative. But for all the time that she was escaping into a bottle, she wasn't present. This made us prematurely self-reliant: you have to 'parent' your parents when they are drunk, compensating for their incapacities.

My view when I look back is that what we children needed was not more 'looking after' than we got. We weren't lacking anything really important in the level of care as *working for* that

99

we had from my parents; what we lacked was care as *being with*. The former care was present in that we were fed and met from the school bus and so on; it was the scarcity of the latter that was the damaging part. And it is for this reason that the widespread assumption that care means the same as 'looking after' needs to be given a second thought. We can care simply by our presence, and it is often the most precious kind of care.

Coda

The underlying claim of this chapter will, I hope, have become clear by now. Care is not *just* 'activity' that does certain things on another's behalf – though it *can* be that too. It need not be goal-governed, and it cannot always be measured by clear outcomes. It is not just *working for*. There is an element of the gratuitous about care. It is non-instrumental. It sees a value in abiding for its own sake. Care is itself, as a *'way'*, also its own *'end'*.

Or, perhaps better, care is a way of abiding whose justification is free of utilitarian or instrumental-izing justifications because it is for *God's* sake, and God is not an end like any other. It is unlike the paths that lead to earthly goals, to creaturely ends (like visiting an elderly person so that I can get my Duke of Edinburgh Award, and then ceasing to visit once the Award is successfully added to my CV). The path of care does not give way to anything else, like the ladder that is kicked away when it has been scaled. The creatures cared for in the context of the way of care are not merely means by which we achieve the *telos* of pleasing God.

And yet care can nevertheless and at the same time *be* a form of relationship with God. This is relationship with God *as* care for creatures. On this account, the *telos* of pleasing God, and of being in relationship with God, *is* (and is not just *by way of*) caring for creatures.

There are good and bad ways of caring for creatures, of course, but the knowledge of creatures as *signs* of God is what guarantees our good use of them. It ensures that we do not *overrate* creatures as substitutes for God (who alone is to be enjoyed for himself, and not used). They are signs of, not alternatives to, God. But it also ensures that we do not *underrate* creatures as temporary but dispensable stages to a purer relationship with the immaterial. That itself would be a sort of idolatry:

constructing a false idea of God as *over against* matter, rather than as one who lets matter point to him; one who lets the world be the medium in which we relate to him.

One Lenten practice that would acknowledge this in a simple way – that creatures are signs of God, and that we are pleasing God when we care for God's creatures – is to take more time over certain interactions; to let *being with* be as valuable as whatever other goal it might lead to.

Jesus, as I have said, is the model of Christian care. He gives a relatively rare insight into his emotional state in one of the Gospel readings set for the Second Sunday in Lent, and what he expresses with such passion is the longing of one who *cares* for people – not *because of* but *despite* their deeds; not in service of some longer-term aim but because of their intrinsic value to him. It is an encouraging text to meditate on in the journey though Lent:

> Jerusalem, Jerusalem, the city that kills the
> prophets and stones those who are sent
> to it! How often have I desired to gather
> your children together as a hen gathers her
> brood under her wings... (Luke 13.34)

ABIDING IN RELATIONSHIPS

The figure with whom I want to begin this chapter is a man called Joe Rose, who witnesses a death in the opening chapter of Ian McEwan's novel *Enduring Love*. It is a famously disturbing – though brilliantly gripping – start to a novel. *Enduring Love* is not required reading for the purposes of this book, and the weak-stomached do not need to immerse themselves in McEwan's description of the death. Its crucial aspects for the theme of this chapter are that it involves a *fall*, and that this fall is the consequence of a collective human failure of solidarity.

One of the great theological issues in Christian tradition has been the nature and meaning of 'original sin' – that is to say, the idea that human beings at no point in their lives, even at birth, are outside sin's realm of influence. Sin is generally conceived of in Christian thought as a 'condition' in which all people live, and which their individual choices cannot exempt them from, or put right. Some of the ways that this transmission of the condition of sin have been imagined can seem unpersuasively mechanical – especially the once-prevalent idea that original sin is a sort of sexually transmitted disease, conveyed by the act of procreation which, because it is always marked by a selfish lust, will inevitably pass on the taint of that selfishness. And some of the ways this chain of transmission have been imagined also seem too tied to the belief that there was a literal man called Adam who started it all off, so that modern Christians cannot embrace the concept with a feeling of intellectual honesty. And some people find the idea that even newborn infants are under the power of sin to be counter-intuitive and objectionable.

For all these reasons, Paul's words in the Letter to Romans can appear to be speaking to us across the centuries in rather alien terms:

> For since death came through a human being, the resurrection of the dead has also come through a human being; for as all die in Adam, so all will be made alive in Christ. (1 Corinthians 15.21-22)

Death was given as the wages of sin, but how can one man's action have brought others to sin such that they too deserve these wages (and find themselves in need of Christ's salvation as a consequence)?

It is a huge question, and I do not propose to answer it completely here. I want to do something more modest, which is to show that the idea of being 'downstream' from a sin that compromises all our action is not an impossible idea to imagine, even if a modern person may want to picture it differently from the early Church Fathers, or the scholars of medieval Christendom. Being 'in Adam' is a description of being unavoidably caught in a world which is imperfect in such a way that our action is radically constrained, with the effect that – however hard we try – we cannot ourselves act perfectly. There will be consequences to our actions, intended and unintended, that we cannot police, and there will always be motivations for our behaviour that are not purely conceived.

Ian McEwan, a self-declared atheist, is perhaps a surprising source to turn to for an illustration of so Christian a doctrine, but the opening sequence of his novel is a vivid and powerful meditation on compromised agency; of being in receipt of the failure of another in such a way that one is helplessly embroiled in that failure.

There is a brief 'Eden' moment before the trouble starts. Joe Rose and his partner Clarissa are together in a paradisal setting. It is a beautiful spring day in the Chiltern Hills in southern England, and they are having a picnic. The woman hands the man not an apple but a bottle of wine; but as he takes it from her – just as in Eden – everything changes.

There is what Joe calls a 'beginning' that will also be an 'ending'. They hear a shout. A hot air balloon is in trouble. Its pilot has jumped out to try to secure it, leaving his 10-year-old grandson inside the basket, and the wind is blowing it towards the edge of an escarpment. Five men (including Joe and a passing motorist called John Logan) run to help them by holding the balloon down – each taking a rope. With five of them on the ropes, they are strong enough to control the balloon and keep the boy safe.

But then a freak double-gust of wind introduces a moment of testing.

A mighty fist socked the balloon in two
rapid blows, one-two, the second more
vicious than the first. [...] Suddenly
we were treading the air with all our
weight in the grip of our fists. [...]
We were rising, and the ground was
dropping away as the balloon was pushed
westwards. I knew I had to get my legs
and feet locked round the rope. But the
end of the line reached below my waist
and my grip was slipping. My legs flailed
in the empty air. Every fraction of a
second that passed increased the drop,
and the point must come when to let go
would be impossible or fatal.

In fact, at this stage, with all the men still united
under the balloon, there is still no *must* about
the fatal point, no necessity to the fall. It really
is avoidable. The wind will subside, and the
weight of the men would be sufficient to ensure
that the balloon could come back down to earth
again – even though its drift over the edge of
the escarpment has caused the ground to drop
away from beneath their feet. But then comes
the point at which everything really does become
irreversible. Someone lets go.

107

Hanging a few feet above the Chilterns escarpment, our crew enacted morality's ancient, irresolvable dilemma: us, or me.

Someone said *me*, and then there was nothing to be gained by saying *us*.

The 'vague communality of purpose' which has bound them together is too weak to hold, and in a split second after the first pair of hands lets go (and the balloon jerks upwards in response to the loss of weight) Joe Rose and two others let go too. The fall of one renders all of their positions impossible; 'being good' makes no sense any more. Only John Logan, in whom 'the flame of altruism must have burned a little stronger' stays on his rope, and by then it is too late. He is carried aloft by the balloon until – a tiny figure against the sky – he can hold on no longer, and falls to his death. 'I've never seen such a terrible thing as that falling man', says Joe.

There can be few more vivid illustrations of what it is to find yourself, as I've put it, 'downstream' from an occurrence (in this case, the first letting go) that then makes any action you go on to take into a compromised action – or a deadly one. The men all become implicated absolutely in a failure of community, and not because of any rational choice they have made, but because of something opaque, elusive, and intractable that *precedes* their choices.

The source of the 'original sin' is rendered brilliantly vague in the novel. Joe Rose cannot say who exactly the 'Adam' was in the wake of whose failure they all 'fall' in one way or another.

> I didn't know, nor have I ever discovered,
> who let go first. I'm not prepared to
> accept that it was me. But everyone
> claims not to have been first.

Just as it is not possible to identify the Adam of the Book of Genesis with an historical person (which would anyway be missing the point of that great saga of the origins of the world), so McEwan's fictional 'Adam' cannot be identified as any single one of the five men holding the balloon's ropes. But what is unquestionable is that they all come under the sway of his action; they all end up (as Paul puts it) '*in* Adam'. And:

> [t]he initial conditions, the force and
> the direction of the force, define all the
> consequent pathways...[1]

This chapter is about the challenges and difficulties of abiding in relationships when living in a world that is fallen, and where it is difficult to say 'us' rather than 'me'. There are many situations in life in which it feels as though one is intensely vulnerable to the actions of those around one – as Joe Rose was as he first hung onto the rope and then released it.

Many people do not enjoy that feeling of vulnerability, and as a reaction to it are propelled into a quest for self-sufficiency. But there is no escaping being part of an 'us' – from conception to old age, human beings are dependent creatures, and even when 'me' seems to prevail over 'us', what is probably more truly happening is that I am contributing to a dysfunctional 'us' rather than opting for no 'us' at all. I am doing my bit for a bad 'us' rather than a good 'us'.

I spoke in the last chapter about my experience of working in a hospice environment. One of the patients I nursed while there was a frail man in his early sixties who had no visitors except for his elderly mother; she would sit daily by his bed. The man said almost nothing to any of the hospice staff apart from 'yes' and 'no'. By contrast with almost all of the other patients, he looked at us with suspicion and what seemed like hostility when we approached his bed. Very few words were exchanged even between him and his mother.

The days went by, and within two weeks he was dead. It was at that point that I discovered from one of the other nurses that he had been a member of the notorious Richardson Gang, a criminal gang that operated in and around South London in the 1960s. They achieved less infamy than the Kray Gang, with whom they feuded, but they had similarly brutal methods, working with a combination of physical violence and psychological terror to promote their interests.

It was I think the most lonely death that I witnessed in the time I worked at St Christopher's Hospice, and it seemed to me that the man's death was the cumulative result of a lifetime of personal attrition. Through a combination of circumstance and personal choice, he had travelled a path that required him to feed off his neighbours, expecting only threat from them in return, and anticipating violence with violence.

He lived in a world of menace and potential betrayal, in which alignment with a local warlord, however crooked, must once have seemed the most plausible source of security. Now, in the weakness of his old age, his sources of power and security had gone, but the expectation of danger, hostility, and betrayal remained alive. Each approaching nurse, doctor or chaplain was glared at. He could not or would not communicate. His life had no fullness (not just because he was bed-bound, for – as I often saw – fullness can still mark a person's life even when his or her physical capacities are fading). Unlike many who died in the hospice, he was mentally able and alert; the incapacity was of a different order: a relational incapacity, perhaps. It was an utterly diminished state in which to die.

It would be cheap of me to bandy this around as a cautionary tale, to prove that crime never pays, and that all those who lead a dishonest or cruel life will inevitably die alone and unhappy. One of the curious things about gangs is that they are a form of human society, and have some of the virtues of loyalty, camaraderie, and even self-sacrifice that mark admirable human enterprises as well.

Some criminals go on to write autobiographies and make money and lead comfortable lives with partners and children. Some lives of quiet virtue, meanwhile, still end in lonely anguish. But what this single, obscure death did tell me was that the stakes are high if a life is lived in a systematically violent way, in the form of daily warfare – and that the consequences can be devastating. The sort of 'us' that a gang represents is defined precariously against a much larger social 'us' whose claims it denies and whose assets it raids, and the little 'us' of a gang can reconfigure itself in an instant to cast out this or that person who is perceived as a source of weakness or an object of paranoid suspicion. Its dog-eat-dog ethos makes the criminal gang an 'us' always close to being a mere collection of 'I's. The loneliness of that man's death was not, in other words, only accidentally related to the way he lived his life.

Lives lived openly and trustfully and cooperatively are not, however, easily achieved. Human relationships are like knots tied in the fabric of life, to help it to hold together as a net or web which is sustaining and permits human flourishing – good relationships are a crucial part of what it is to live a life of ordered faithfulness.[2]

But, ironically, they are not usually achieved through will-power alone. An individual decision only goes so far. Just as no one person was able to keep the balloon on the ground in the opening chapter of *Enduring Love*, so it is with many people's attempts to keep their life in a certain sort of shape.

The fragility of those around them, holding the other ropes, is a source of anxiety. The desire for a controlled space which is safe and managed is awakened by this awareness of other people's fragility, and the frightening feeling of vulnerability that goes with it. The gangster who died in the hospice could be seen as just an extreme version of how such fear translates into a desire for intensified control.

In Ecclesiastes 3, the 'Preacher' enumerates the sheer diversity of situations that present themselves to human life in the world:

> For everything there is a season, and a
> time for every matter under heaven: a
> time to be born, and a time to die; a time
> to plant, and a time to pluck up what
> is planted; a time to kill, and a time to

heal; a time to break down, and a time
to build up; a time to weep, and a time
to laugh; a time to mourn, and a time
to dance; a time to throw away stones,
and a time to gather stones together; a
time to embrace, and a time to refrain
from embracing; a time to seek, and a
time to lose; a time to keep, and a time
to throw away; a time to tear, and a time
to sew; a time to keep silence, and a time
to speak; a time to love, and a time to
hate; a time for war, and a time for peace.
(Ecclesiastes 3.1-8)

It is an extraordinary catalogue. Everything is
beautiful in its own time and place, whether that
experience over there, or this task over here.

It is interesting to contrast the litany of paired
contrasts in Ecclesiastes with the vows that are
made in a Christian marriage service.

I take you to be my husband/wife,
to have and to hold
from this day forward;
for better, for worse,
for richer, for poorer,

115

in sickness and in health,
to love and to cherish,
till death us do part;
according to God's holy law.
In the presence of God I make this vow.[3]

Wedding vows too acknowledge that there will be different times when different things will happen: times of better, and times of worse; times of richness and times of poverty; times of sickness and times of health, and so on. It sounds very Ecclesiastes-like.

But there is one important difference between the Ecclesiastes passage and the marriage vows. One is a description, and the second is a response. The first seems simply to *describe* all the different moments scattered through human experience; the other undertakes to *bind* them together. Ecclesiastes is a *list*; the vows are a *project*, a *venture*, the anticipation of a *story*. Instead of resting with a world of disjointed fragments, with the observation that there are some things over here, some things over there, and that sometimes this happens, sometimes that, the promises of bride and bridegroom undertake to try to make the fragments part of a meaningful whole; to frame these disparate experiences in a shared life; to thread them together, one to another, by their faithfulness and love.

The Christian belief is that where there is love, and the binding of persons *in* love, then there is also a binding of time, a shaping of something that is more than the sum of its different parts. Love like this will not be what Shakespeare in Sonnet 116 calls 'Time's fool'.[4] It will be time's *artist*. And what is true of marriage in a particularly sacramental way is true of all committed human relationships; they seek to foster bonds that will be sustainable through time, taking time as their medium, and working with its texture to fashion something that has a unity and a beauty to it. They work to translate 'me' into 'us' in a way that it has more to it than the shifting allegiances of the gang.

The practices that bind a human relationship across its lifetime are practices of *abiding*. Binding is *achieved* by abiding, and relationships that abide – to recall the Shakespeare sonnet a second time – can 'look on tempests and not be shaken'.[5] And this seems to offer an occasion to think about one of Jesus's parables – one in which a

117

storm also features and in which abiding is also a
theme: the parable of the houses built upon sand
and upon rock.

> 'Everyone then who hears these words
> of mine and acts on them will be like a
> wise man who built his house on rock.
> The rain fell, the floods came, and the
> winds blew and beat on that house, but it
> did not fall, because it had been founded
> on rock. And everyone who hears these
> words of mine and does not act on them
> will be like a foolish man who built his
> house on sand. The rain fell, and the
> floods came, and the winds blew and beat
> against that house, and it fell – and great
> was its fall!' (Matthew 7.24-27)

In a moment I am going to ask how this parable
might illuminate something about the character
of the relationships that Christians are called to
make. But first, I need to acknowledge a personal
challenge in writing this chapter. It's a challenge
of which I am acutely conscious, because I am a
person who has been through a divorce and who
has subsequently remarried. Indeed, it could quite
reasonably be concluded that I have no business

writing about the importance of abiding at all, and that is a point of view I would understand.

However, the experience of having a failed marriage (or – to put it more accountably – of *failing in marriage*) has confronted me with a set of challenges and insights that I hold very important.

A broken relationship is a spiritual failure, but so is a celebration of human determination as the solution to all of life's trials. The embrace of an ideal of perseverance *can* be a form of destructive self-reliance. By contrast, the exposure to shame or grief that ensues when a well-managed life falls apart *can* – at the same time, and without negating the pain and cost – be an occasion of grace. While it will not automatically do so, such exposure can lead to a life in which there is a greater acknowledgement of one's need, vulnerability, and dependence on God and on other human beings.

I argued earlier that tying secure knots in the fabric of our lives by means of human relationships is both a deeply valuable thing – permitting ordered faithfulness – but at the same time something that cannot be achieved by the exercise of mere willpower. The rock in Jesus's parable, to be sure, seems initially like the perfect image of something that *abides*, and as a consequence the perfect image of what people need to be like if they're to have good relationships. If Ecclesiastes shows us how fragmentary the world can seem, how elusive and changeable, how like shifting sand, then we can be forgiven for thinking that *rock* is surely the solution. Rocks don't change; they are always the same. Rocks are secure, tough and predictable.

Modern Western people are often quite drawn to the idea that they are at their best when they and their lives are rock-like; when they are self-reliant and self-guaranteeing. Abiding, on this model, is achieved by steady determination, or by finding a corner of the world where life's vicissitudes cannot touch you. Otherwise, the world will slip from beneath your feet, like so much sand. One could read the parable of the houses on rock and on sand and think that that's what Jesus Christ is commending.

But the theme of this chapter has been that willpower cannot achieve everything in a fallen world (this is what Joe Rose and John Logan discover), and that there are risks in seeking artificial protection against it in the form of some human power (like the power of the Richardson Gang). This is, after all, the Jesus who teaches his followers not to plan too carefully for tomorrow; the Jesus who invites his hearers to consider the lilies of the field and the birds of the air, which do not exercise control over things, or manage their environments, but are wholly reliant on a larger environment which God's grace alone sustains. They live receivingly from God's bounty. They know what it is to be dependent.

So the parable of the houses on rock and sand may not be best read as telling its listeners that their cleverness and industry will solve all their problems. It's not just a big celebration of their technical skills of building. It's not saying that life is all about the choice of a good site and, after that, sitting tight. The rock in the parable may stand for a *totally different* sort of abiding. And to our worried eyes it may actually look more like sand than rock.

That is because, from one perspective, what Jesus seems to be teaching is an abiding not of self-sufficiency but of radical relationship with *others*

121

in the context of radical relationship with *God*, of *covenant*, which means deep and sometimes frightening self-surrender. Our deepest rock is found when we abide not *in* ourselves but *beyond* ourselves, in relationship with God and with others; when security is not fortified sameness, but a willingness to confront challenge and change, trusting that, by God's grace and not an embattled entrenchment, our relationships can adapt as we move through the surprises of time.

It may seem odd to propose 'covenant' as a mode of relationship that could actually have the effect of dismantling some of the things a person has decided or determined for himself. It may seem positively dangerous to suggest that sometimes a call to life predicated more fully on God's grace might entail the coming apart of promises or commitments that one has made in the past. But if all that makes a human relationship work is human *will*, then it is founded on very uncertain ground indeed.

Human beings are prone at every turn to construct bad forms of interdependence, in which we make others the 'raw material' of our own identities, or conspire in others' perceptions of us in order to ground a sense of our own reality and value. If these sorts of relationships succeed in achieving a certain sort of fixity, it is a brittle one: they are houses built on sand.

Covenant relationships are not about wanting others to be instances of our favourite stereotype, or trying to *be* the favourite stereotype of someone else. As the North American theologian David Kelsey says,[6] locating one's reality and value in humanly-grounded constructions of 'reciprocal dependency' will fail, because:

> [W]e absorb [others] into our project of securing our reality and value, dissolving their otherness to us and defining them as extensions of ourselves, but only at the price of being conscripted into their projects, eroding our own otherness to them.

The true ground of our personal identity is our covenant relationship with God, in which we are not an instrument of God's will, and God cannot be an instrument of ours; in which a focus on 'will' is relativized by 'trust in a genuinely eccentric ground' of the reality and value of who we are. This centre is beyond ourselves (it is 'eccentric'), because it is in God.

But that is more easily said than learnt, and for as long as history lasts, we will continue at some level to live 'in Adam'. The Pelagian response to sin (a response that has been touched on before in this book) may argue that greater moral effort can remedy the problem, but this is to keep the human will centre stage and resist the 'eccentricity' in which human creatures find their real value. Orthodox Christian teaching argues instead that human good works are only ever responses to a prior grace, and are learnt in the context of a radical dependency on such grace.

It is a curious thing, but some of life's most impressive people – people who have many competencies, and abundant resources of strength, determination and self-sufficiency – may have to take bigger steps than some other people in order to find the rock that is 'abiding', the rock that abides not statically but shiftingly and transformingly. They will find this rock in the mode of self-loss, and in the framework of 'eccentric' relationship. It is *covenant* rock, and a capacity for self-surrender – often hard to acquire – is what enables a person to find it.

This is not to say that the Christian life is one of complete passivity, in which the disciple is to cast herself adrift in a rudderless boat and let the currents of life take her where they will. That would make it nonsensical even to *try* to live under vows, or seek to bind the fragments of lived life into meaningful wholes; it would mock quests for stability like those of the Benedictine monk or promises of faithfulness like those made by the partners to a marriage.

The Christian life is not one of passivity, but of living from resources one does not own, which means relinquishing a certain sort of sovereignty. The Benedictine monk does this by (for example) holding possessions in common, and being obedient to a collectively-discerned will. The married person does this by (for example) unlearning habits of defensiveness and pride. The Christian life means learning to be a good 'us' not a bad 'us', by embracing patterns of relationship that respond well to contingency and the unexpected, so that when the balloon goes up enough people stay holding the ropes. Sometimes the patterns of relationship Christians (like any other human beings) evolve for themselves do *not* respond well to contingency or the unexpected, and new patterns have, with difficulty, to be learnt instead.

Central to the Church's ministry are practices that honour decision, but these are set alongside practices that deal with the limits and failures of decision. Clergy preside over the great moments of adult choice (confirmations and marriages, for example), but they are also charged with the task of helping people to deal with the ways in which their choices are outrun by novelty, interruption, mistakes, surprises, and so on.

Very often, the reason that non-regular church-goers find themselves in a church is because of the baptism of an infant or because of a death. Both are moments of being overwhelmed.

However planned a pregnancy may be, there is always something gratuitous, superadded and irruptive about a new birth, in which those most closely involved feel the limits of their own control and their call to receive a gift that comes from outside them.

And in death, a person's self-possession is radically relinquished and those left behind commend them to a mercy and a gracious keeping that – once again – is beyond their control; there is nothing else they can do.

The baptism of *adult* believers is a conscious surrender to what is often a literal overwhelming: an immersion in a death like Christ's that will lead to a new and decentred life *in* Christ. The practices of confession and absolution, meanwhile, are part of the pattern of regular churchgoers' lives, and these too (like the eucharist, which is among other things food for a pilgrimage) are a God-given resource for lives which personal choices cannot ever fully regulate; medicine for life after the Fall. Day in and day out, they proclaim the mystery that human beings are not in command of their lives. People do not live by will alone; the rock that is their security is of another kind.

As David Ford proposed in a Lent Book some years ago,[7] the Christian life involves learning to be overwhelmed well, and this will mean in the company of others, in the body of a church that weans its members from an idolatrous fixation on their own virtues – that weans them, in other words, from a Pelagian alternative whose symbol might perhaps be the stiff upper lip, and whose resolute determination not to weaken can often mask a fear of what such weakness might entail.

Human relationships are as fragile and as in need of grace as newborn infants and departing souls. They will be handled better when this is acknowledged. God provides for their care in a way that resembles his provision for the newly born and the newly dead – in the new form of life which Christ founded on the wobbly and shifting 'rock' which was Peter, and in the sacraments and practices that constitute that form of life.

Human relationships will sometimes fail – often in small ways and occasionally in big and terrible ways. The Christian confidence is that no failure that is enacted by the embroiled human will can outrun grace. The Christian belief is that our abiding in relationship with God and one another is a 'work' that prospers only because God first abides in relationship with us. And God can bind all things – including the times, the seasons and our fractured lives – not because God is one solitary and almighty *will*, but because he is faithful, and makes covenants, and *gives* himself, making an 'us' that will abide for eternity because it is established in the power of this infinitely responsive love.

Coda

[A]bsolutely speaking, the angels arc more
to the image of God than man is, but […]
in some respects man is more like to God.[8]

These are the words of the great medieval
theologian, St Thomas Aquinas, in his thirteenth-
century masterwork the *Summa Theologiae*. He is
addressing the topic of 'Whether the angels arc
more to the image of God than man is?'. It may
seem a rather rarefied question, but it is closely
related to what has been the core concern of this
chapter – as is Thomas's answer.

There is no fragility to the angels' calling to serve
God. They are wholly identified with the tasks
thcy perform, and they perform them perfectly,
usually bodilessly, and without the interference of
a sinful will. They are 'intellectual natures', which
means that they do not require bodies; they are
pure spirit. They also, and for the same reason,
do not generate new life from their relations with
one another. They do not procreate.

In their permanence and their immaterial natures,
Thomas admits that the angels have a special

advantage over human beings. They can be an image of God's unchanging constancy. The human condition, which is a mixed or compound nature, made up of both intellect and bodiliness (and having a fallen will), is, as the Letter to Hebrews puts it, 'lower than the angels' (Hebrews 2.9). So in these important respects, human being is a less adequate image of God than angelic being. It belongs to a chancy world in which there is always a gap between intention and action, as also between action and result (recall Paul's lament that 'I do not do the good I want, but the evil I do not want is what I do' (Romans 7.19); a world in which each person is also vulnerably dependent on others for living his or her life meaningfully and well.

Vulnerably dependent, but by the same token, *extraordinary*. For human beings, in their mixed natures, have the advantage over angels that they must relate to one another to be themselves. A human being must be part of an 'us' in order ever to be an 'I'. In particular, they *do* procreate. And in this respect, they are a better image of one key aspect of God's nature of which the angels cannot so adequately be an image: God's covenant nature; God's commitment to relationship; and

130

the fact that God too *is God* only by a sort of generation. This relational being is the aspect of God so well attested by one of the readings for the Third Sunday of Lent: 'I will make with you an everlasting covenant, my steadfast, sure love for David' (Isaiah 55.3b).

Jesus Christ became incarnate. In taking to himself the life of a creature, God did not assume an angelic nature, but a human one. His taking on humanity may have bound God to a nature that was, as one commentator puts it 'inferior to the nature of the angels, in terms of degrees of perfection'. But despite that, the same commentator remarks, 'humans are higher than the angels in respect to reflecting God's relational behavior':

> Because human nature is inclined toward persons 'proceeding' from persons, much like the spiration of the Holy Spirit from the interpersonal communion of the Father and the Son, Aquinas concludes that humans reflect God's relational qualities more deeply than the angels, even though the angels reflect God's immaterial essence more intensely.[9]

If the Son of God becomes human and not angelic, then the flawed but social human is given a unique intimacy with the divine nature, through Christ. Indeed, the fragility that goes with being a relational being is also the ground for the gift of the *imago dei* – the image of God in people – which in turn permits God's participation in human nature in the incarnation, and human nature's consequent participation in God. Human beings, struggling with the challenge of being an 'us', are in fact communing with an aspect of God's nature that is kept back from the angels. This is perhaps why the Epistle of Peter writes that the Gospel announces 'things into which angels long to look' (1 Peter 1.12):

> Angels can never experience being
> 'clothed with Christ' in baptism (Gal
> 3.27) or 'bear[ing] the image of the
> man of heaven' (1 Cor 15.49), being a
> member of Christ bodily (1 Cor 6.15),
> or being the 'temple of God/Holy Spirit'
> within one's nature (1 Cor 3.16, 6.19).
> The word became flesh, not angelic,
> and because of this humanity is offered
> a deeper communion with God's nature
> than even the angels.[10]

The fragility of human relating often causes human beings to fall, but it is the ground of the special way in which humans are intimate with God. This is a worthy subject both for reflection and thankfulness.

'I will make with you an everlasting covenant.'

ABIDING IN EXILE

In the previous chapter, the theme of abiding became complexified by the discussion of sin and grace. On the one hand, and following the emphasis of the chapters on stability, contemplation, and care, there was a continued exploration of abiding as something that Christians are called to *do* – specifically, in this case, in their personal relationships.

The Christian vocation involves trying to stitch together the fragments of lived experience in all the changes and chances of this fleeting world in order to make something meaningful from them: to live lives that are signs of the faithful God who abides eternally. But at the same time, the chapter focussed on the limits of willpower, and the mysterious fact that God's call to abide involves a kind of relinquishment of control, a plunge into uncertainty, and a sometimes difficult education in the value of openness.

Certain human relationships can become embodiments of determined fixity in a way that opposes this learnt openness. In this sense, the chapter uncovered another perspective on Christian abiding, one of which Jesus's teaching also makes a good deal: the view of abiding as something that Christians are called to *receive*. We first receive God's abiding-with-us (which is often mediated through other creatures with whom we share the world). And although often we will find this experience of God's faithfulness awakening our answering response and a readiness in us to mirror that faithfulness, equally, sometimes, this experience of God's faithfulness will only be had when we first lose our powers of control.

The US theologian Stanley Hauerwas, following his teacher John Howard Yoder, has said that the Christian life ought always to be a 'life lived out of control'.

> To live 'out of control' [...] is to renounce the illusion that our task as Christians is to make history come out right. [...] Rather, we believe that a more truthful account of what is really going on in the world comes from those who are 'out of control.' For those who are without control have fewer illusions

about what makes this world secure or
safe and they inherently distrust those
who say they are going to help through
power and violence.[1]

The second half of this book will have a slightly
different emphasis from the first half, because it
will be concerned with the apparently paradoxical
relationship of abiding to just such 'out-of-
controlness'. It is in learning the right ways to
be 'out of control' that Christians recognize
that abiding is never just a human achievement
– or, at least, can only be thought of as a human
achievement when its source lies in God.

Angels have made their appearance in this book
already, in the 'Coda' which ended the previous
chapter. And the character who I want to preside
over the opening of this chapter is as it happens
an angel: Damiel, played by Bruno Ganz in
Wim Wenders' 1997 film *Wings of Desire* (or, in
German, *Der Himmel über Berlin*).

The film is remarkably true to the Thomist view
of angels as pure spirits, or intellectual beings.
Damiel first appears as one of a multitude of
angels who move unseen amongst the populace of

a still-divided Berlin. The walls that keep people's lives and thoughts apart – the psychological walls and not just the physical ones that have their supreme instance in the fault line through the middle of the city – are not an obstacle to the angels. They are able to hear the inner thoughts, the fears, hopes, desires and memories of the people they watch over. They are calm, compassionate, largely silent, and in this sense they are exemplars of a certain sort of *changeless* abiding.

Their task, as it is articulated in a conversation between Damiel and another angel, Cassiel, at one point in the film, is to 'assemble, testify, preserve'. They look and listen for whatever in people's actions or thoughts is beautiful, noble, high-minded, generous, or creative, and they garner it by their witness, ensuring that it has a place in the eternity they inhabit.

But a key turning point in the film is Damiel's emerging desire to shed his wings; to exchange the abiding of 'assembly' and 'preservation' – the abiding of being always in control, always the same ('unresting, unhasting', to quote a famous Scottish hymn[2]) – for another sort of abiding: the abiding of making a home, in the midst of the world. This desire is precipitated by his falling in love with a lonely trapeze artist over whom he watches, but it is more broadly also a falling in love with the *world* – precisely in its 'out-of-controlness'. It is a longing to live at the mercy of forces and eventualities that cannot be foreseen, because that seems to be more like real *living*.

> It's grand to live by the spirit, to testify for
> eternity only what is spiritual in people's
> minds. But sometimes I'm fed up with
> my spiritual existence of forever hovering
> above. I'd like to feel a weight in me, to
> end the infinity, and to tie me to earth.
> I'd like at each step, each gust of wind, to
> be able to say: 'Now', 'now', and 'now';
> no longer 'forever' and 'for eternity'. To
> sit at the empty place at a card table, be
> greeted, even if only by a nod.

At this point, Damiel recalls a series of Scriptural accounts in which the intervention of angels is recorded, including Jacob's wrestling at Jabbok Ford in Genesis 32, Tobias's journey with the angel in the Apocrypha (Book of Tobit 6), and Abraham's and Sarah's hospitality to three angelic visitors in Genesis 18:

On every occasion that we participated, it
was a pretence. Wrestling, allowing a hip
to be put out – in pretence. Catching a
fish – in pretence. In pretence, sitting at
tables; drinking and eating in pretence.
Having lambs roasted and wine served in
the tents in the desert only in pretence.
I don't have to beget a child or plant
a tree, but it would be nice, coming
home after a long day, to feed the cat
like Philip Marlowe... to have a fever...
blackened fingers from the newspaper. To
be excited not only by the mind but by
a meal; by the line of a neck, by an ear.
To lie! In one's teeth! As you're walking,
to feel your bones moving along. At
last to guess instead of always knowing.
To be able to say: 'Ah!', and 'Oh!', and
'Hey!'...

This passage is a paean of praise to the changeable
world; a litany of the beauty of limits, in which
(in a delicious reversal of that human instinct to
eradicate all uncertainty and know everything
fully, clearly and precisely) the angel longs to
put away knowledge in favour of the joy of
guessing. The created world's transience makes it

an apt place in which to appreciate the wonder of discovery, reciprocity, particularity.

Cassiel's guarded response to Damiel's longing to 'take up residence' in the world (one sort of abiding) is to invoke the virtue of 'keeping things the same' (another sort of abiding). 'Remain alone', he counsels. 'Remain serious... remain spirit... remain at a distance... keep your word'. Each verb is '*bleiben*', the German word for abide.

Damiel's eventual choice is willingly to embrace permanent exile from the calm eternity of angelic life, because he wants a home in the changing world where humans live in time. His angelic home grows to feel like a sort of exile from the world he longs to inhabit, and his voluntary exile in the world emerges as a sort of home in which he can really be happy.

Exile is the theme of this chapter. The Bible – New Testament as much as Old – is riddled with the language of home, but drenched in the experience of exile. The biblical paradigm of the man, or woman, of God is of one who has no home soil on which to stand, and only the Lord's unchanging nature to cling to. We see this paradigm embodied again and again from the expulsion of Adam and Eve onwards, in Abraham, Joseph, Moses, Ruth, Jeremiah, Ezekiel, right the way through to John the Seer on the island of Patmos. 'Home is where the Lord is'. Which if it means everywhere also means nowhere, for there is no specific place to lay your head that is in itself the fixed and permanent and *right* place.

It may not be all that peculiar to think and talk constantly of home when you don't actually have one. It is perhaps like thinking about food when you're hungry. And maybe that explains perfectly well why the Bible circles endlessly around ideas of home when home is so elusive for the people whose story it is. But what we find in some parts of the Bible is something that seems rather more paradoxical. There are texts that don't simply remind us that we all long for what we don't have. They say that God's people *have* what they long for in *not* having it. They have it in one way by not having it in another. They are home *when* they are in exile, not just afterwards.

The opening chapters of the Book of Acts show us the battered frame of Stephen, the first Christian martyr, whose earthly exile is displayed in the stones that rain down upon him. The message of those stones is that there is no place for him in this world, and no place for people like him. In this sense, we glimpse in him again the paradigmatic biblical human being. And yet in exactly this moment of expulsion he looks up into heaven, full of the Holy Ghost, and sees the glory of God embracing him. In that *transitus* – as he is cast out of the earthly city – he is conformed to Christ, who is his true home. And Christ is with him, and he is with Christ. In all the riot and commotion and fury – in all that movement – his gaze is described as 'steadfast'; as able to dwell on the unchanging vision of God. His gaze is at rest. He has somewhere to abide.

Meanwhile Saul stands, like an unwitting Elisha looking on at the ascent of Elijah, little knowing what mantle is about to fall upon his own shoulders. For Saul like Stephen will shortly make his own *transitus* – his own journey. Not to heaven (yet), but to a new status as *Paul*. What we will shortly see in his case is another sort of dispossession – not merely of city or of life (though he loses both of these in due course), but of a particular sort of religious certainty.

Saul stands looking on at Stephen with a set of givens in place: clear moral and Scriptural reference points. This is not the special preserve of the Pharisee. Feeling oneself to be a possessor of such givens is not an unfamiliar feeling for Christians either. There are plenty of Christian theologians who talk of what we have been *given* in Christ as providing us with all we need to order our lives. Scripture, sacraments, the liturgy, the tradition – these givens stock our Christian knapsacks and we need only dig into those knapsacks to find just the right thing for each occasion.

Saul perhaps has a confidence analogous to that. But in Stephen's death and the events that ensue, his givens – his *truth* – are about to be challenged by new findings. *Given things* will come up against *found things*, and the found things will need to be judged by him as to whether they are of God or not. And if they are, *he* will need to change as his understanding of *them* changes, in order to achieve a new integration of the found with the given.

The Gospel of John contains what is perhaps one of the top ten most quotable lines in the New

Testament – a slogan emblazoned on thousands of church billboards along with 'God so loved the world...' and 'Repent ye, for the Kingdom of Heaven is at hand'. It is: 'I am the Way, the Truth and the Life: no man cometh to the Father, but by me'. This seems a sure-fire recipe for Christian exclusivism and certain possession of the truth – a text about givens. Or so it seems.

I do not want to deny that it is a text of assurance. But it's a much more complicated text than it is allowed to be by the uses to which it is put. It is regularly used as a text about proprietorship (inasmuch as 'given' things are for us 'possessed' things). On this account, it is telling us Christians about 'our Jesus', as I've sometimes rather disturbingly heard him called in sermons. It's celebrated as a text about *our* Word of God, and most of all *our* salvation. But that is to miss the ways in which it is a text of *dis*possession.

It points us not so much back to what we have already been given in Christ, but forward to what we have yet to *find*. Indeed, the implication of this text is that *a constant and never-ending finding* is the mode of our possession of Christ, and that such possession is better described as following. We can be at home in him, we can have our abode in him, only by constantly receiving a future in which the Holy Spirit delivers him to us *again*. By living 'now', and 'now', and 'now', as Damiel puts it; and by saying 'Ah!' and 'Oh!' and 'Hey!'.

It's a truism that modern Western notions of truth – whether through the fault of the Greeks or the philosophers of the Enlightenment – are centred on precise, transparent (and therefore fully-possessed) meanings. But less important than establishing who is to blame for making us think that real truth is clear, fixed and timeless is realizing that we do, and that it's a problem. I suspect our tendency when we hear that Jesus is the Way, the Truth and the Life is to make what *he* means by 'Way' and by 'Life' (modes of finding) into something that resembles what *we* mean by 'Truth' (a mode of givenness).

But Jesus spoke Aramaic, and the word he is most likely to have used when he talked of himself as the 'Truth' is the Aramaic version of the Hebrew word 'Amen'. And the word 'Amen' doesn't imply a given, possessed item of propositional truth; its meaning is most naturally a relational one, and it

146

means 'reliability'. When you say 'Amen' at the end of a prayer, you are saying something like 'I rely on this', or 'here is something (or someone) you can rely on'. Which is to place the idea of truth back into lived life and the processes by which our faith is tried and tested as faithfulness and not as a body of doctrine.

Jesus is one to be followed with utter confidence. His love is unfailing. And our challenge when faced with this heavily-freighted verse of John's Gospel is to reverse the usual flow, and to make what we have come to mean by 'Truth' more like what we understand by 'Way' and by 'Life'. It is to make given things more responsive to found things; the life of possession more a life of apocalypse (or *unveiling*). This is Truth that is *like* Way; more than that, it is Truth *as* Way. We do not sit still and, Gollum-like, cradle this Truth. We inhabit it, and are at home in it, by moving forward into it; by finding and re-finding it.

One implication of this is that Christians may be nearer to God when they are in some sort of exile than when they are not. Or, to recall an even more radical idea that has already suggested itself in this chapter, it is that they need to be in exile in order to be truly 'at home' – just as the angel Damiel found a sense of homecoming as he went out into a changeable world that he could not control. 'We have no abiding city', says the Letter to Hebrews (13.14).

And Jeremiah is the greatest Old Testament exponent of the fact that there are some vocations you can only find when you are – literally – in exile. In his case, the exile in question is the exile of the Jewish people in Babylon. In the eyes of many of the people who were undergoing it, this condition can only have appeared an unmitigated disaster. It must have seemed that the loss of a clearly defined space of agency and identity – the loss of a defended land and a walled city and a centralized cult – meant an absolute withdrawal of God's favour, and left nothing to be done except lament.

But Jeremiah the prophet sees a different possi-bility – to make this 'prison' into a 'way', a calling, the realization of something new about God and the service of God in the world.

These are the words of the letter that the prophet Jeremiah sent from Jerusalem to

the remaining elders among the exiles,
and to the priests, the prophets, and
all the people, whom Nebuchadnezzar
had taken into exile from Jerusalem to
Babylon. [...] It said: Thus says the Lord
of hosts, the God of Israel, to all the
exiles whom I have sent into exile from
Jerusalem to Babylon: Build houses and
live in them; plant gardens and eat what
they produce. Take wives and have sons
and daughters; take wives for your sons,
and give your daughters in marriage,
that they may bear sons and daughters;
multiply there, and do not decrease. But
seek the welfare of the city where I have
sent you into exile, and pray to the Lord
on its behalf, for in its welfare you will
find your welfare. (Jeremiah 29.1, 4-7)

This is an astonishingly affirmative response to
an unprecedented experience of exile, and it
is this memory that is at work, I think, in the
Christian ethics of those like Stanley Hauerwas
and John Howard Yoder who commend exile
– or life lived 'out of control', which is to say,
without a compulsion to hold all the strings of
power – as a good way of walking with God. It

149

is its own response to the question posed in the Psalms: 'How could we sing the LORD's song in a foreign land?' (Psalm 137.4).

That strange and rebellious psalm, Psalm 137, offers *its* answer – it sings a song of resistance, as if to say: 'you asked for a song; well, see how you like this', and it ends on a note of notoriously violent anger. But that is only one possible answer. Jeremiah suggests something less confrontational and more 'over-accepting', like the teaching that the best way to respond to being wronged is to do good in return. ('Love your enemies, do good to those who hate you, bless those who curse you, pray for those who abuse you' (Luke 6.27); 'if your enemies are hungry, feed them; if they are thirsty, give them something to drink; for by doing this you will heap burning coals on their heads' (Romans 12.20-21)). He proposes: 'Seek the welfare of the city'.

Jeremiah says, in other words, that there are ways of being a blessing to those around you that are less like hosting than they are like *being a good guest*. Admittedly, in Chapter 1 of this book, the virtue of stability was celebrated because it makes it possible to offer *hospitality* to one's environment, and in Chapter 3, '*hosting*' was held up as a privileged mode of care – but it is possible to set alongside them the value of witnessing to God in a context that is managed by someone else: by *another* person or community.

Even Benedict's *Rule*, for all its emphasis on stability, preserved something of this insight. It acknowledged that there is a Christ-likeness to being a guest *of* the monastery as well as a host *at* the monastery (Christ after all performed both roles, and his first disciples were sent out on the road mainly in order to be guests). The Benedictine practice of hospitality gives a high status to the one who arrives from outside, and allows the visiting outsider to associate with the monks in a way that was not always the case in other orders. As one Benedictine commentator notes:

> Monks and guests are two faces of
> Christ: one opens and gives; the other
> knocks and makes himself a beggar. The
> monastery is the house of God because of
> this perfect presence of Christ as all in all,
> in the one who welcomes and in the one
> who is received.[3]

The monk in community may be seeking to imitate Christ, but the itinerant is *also* Christ. People who arrive as outsiders can bear important insights and provoke important challenges; they can be a blessing by being a critical force. In their persons, the 'givens' of the monastery get confronted with something (or more accurately, someone) 'newly found'. Outsiders can point things out to the community that it needs to hear, and help it to come to a better understanding of itself and its present calling.

So, despite Benedict's concern about the dangers of the wandering 'gyrovague', his *Rule* still allows a recognition of other forms of Christian witness than life within the enclosure; there is an ecology of callings, in which those who travel also have value. Wider Christian tradition has held fast to this insight too. It has a deep belief that one of the best ways to imagine Christian discipleship is as pilgrimage.

This idea can be found in the desert Fathers, in the Celtic tradition of monasticism, in the self-understanding of Catholic and Protestant missionaries, and in many other guises. Such lives 'incarnate the attitude that the Christian is a stranger and nomad on earth, in search of the real homeland' (cf. Hebrews 11.13-16).[4] The gyrovagues Benedict talks about may be a perversion of this type of disciple, but this does not discredit the type as such.

The pilgrimage model says that certain sorts of Christian wisdom can only be learnt 'in a foreign country', so to speak – when in constant exile. And in a curious way, this vision complements Benedict's even while it seems to be its mirror image. This is because, for Benedict, staying in one place is a *means* to spiritual progress or 'travel'. It is, so to speak, staying still in order to journey towards God. In the words of the *Rule*:

> with hearts expanded in love's
> indescribable sweetness, we run along
> the path of God's commands so that,
> never turning away from his instruction
> and persevering in his doctrine in the
> monastery until death, through patience
> we may share the sufferings of Christ and
> also deserve to be sharers in his kingdom.[5]

Meanwhile, the life of being a stranger and pilgrim upon earth – enacting one's status as an

153

exile – is a way of finding where one's true and abiding home is, by living dependently on God. The sense of an ecology of vocations emerges again: for some the knowledge of the special sort of home God offers needs to be discovered in having no permanent resting place in this world, and for some the discovery of God's infinitely new and transforming horizons is best achieved by staying still. As Michael Paternoster says, some people need to stay where God puts them, even if they feel like moving, and some people must move when God requires them to, even if they feel like staying.[6]

If this is a Christian wisdom, it was a Jewish one first, and modern Christians have much to learn from the Jewish experience of exile, and in particular from Jeremiah's advice to be ready to view exile as a gift and not an absolute evil. While not exactly the role of a 'guest', the condition of an exile can give a context in which to live out a vocation, to be a blessing to a 'host culture', and in doing so to draw nearer to the knowledge of God.

The Hebrew word *Shechinah* means 'dwelling', or 'that which dwells'. It is the Hebrew word that is most apt for describing God's presence, or God's abiding, with his people. Although the word does not appear directly in the Old Testament, it is often to be encountered in other Jewish literature, and its sense is quite definitely derived from the Bible's descriptions of God's presence. The *Shechinah* is what moves before the people of Israel in the Exodus from Egypt, in the form of the pillar of cloud by day and of fire by night. The *Shechinah* is what then, after Sinai, dwells in the moving tabernacle in the desert, where the Ark of the Covenant is kept. And the *Shechinah* is the glory that resides eventually in the Temple of Solomon in Jerusalem. It stays put when the people need to stay put, and it moves when they need to move.

And it is precisely this latter idea that is most striking and most important for the purposes of this chapter: the very remarkable idea of a *presence* (or an *abiding*) *that moves*:

> The Lord went in front of them in a
> pillar of cloud by day, to lead them along
> the way, and in a pillar of fire by night, to
> give them light, so that they might travel
> by day and by night. (Exodus 13.21)

155

This is, as Jürgen Moltmann has said, a 'good symbol for the mobilizing presence of God in history'.[7] God dwells with the Israelites all the time, but God is also moving all the time. He is always before them, but by having God always before them, they find *themselves* moving. God dwells among the Israelites as a 'Trailblazer', says Moltmann.[8]

The prologue of John's Gospel – in a much discussed phrase – describes the Word's becoming flesh as a 'tabernacling' amongst us. God's 'glory' (the Greek word here is *doxa*) finds yet another way to dwell: in the holy of holies that is Christ's body. The glory of God about which John's Gospel is speaking is, of course, the *Shechinah* once again. And this fleshly tabernacle, although compared explicitly in the New Testament with the Temple, can also be compared with something even more provisional. Although English translations more often than not render the 'tabernacling' of the Word made flesh in John 1 as 'dwelling', the resonances of the original Greek are with a specific *sort* of dwelling: it is the sort you might do in a *tent*.

The US artist Dayton Castleman brought this out vividly in an artwork entitled *Caravan*. The piece was a model of a modern trailer caravan, its windows lit from within, that was placed on the altar of a church, in the place where (in many churches) a highly decorated 'tabernacle' for the reservation of consecrated bread might be found.[9]

Christ's dwelling amongst his people is, like the caravan in the artwork, really *amongst* us. It is a dwelling-in-the-midst – like the one that Damiel the angel chooses to embrace – rather than confinement to a distant, changeless sphere. It is dwelling in a provisional, moveable space that is tent-like, or even caravan-like; which can be uprooted and repitched in a way that is responsive to circumstance and to environment. It is the enactment of perfect love in a world of gusts of wind and moving limbs and roasted lamb. In Moltmann's words, we can imagine this 'Christ-room' as:

> [A] moved and moving room and, in
> view of the kingdom of God the Father
> (1 Cor 15:28), as a room open to the
> future, an 'ante-room'.[10]

This abiding God shows us the deep meaning of what it is to be at home, and this 'at-homeness'

157

is quite compatible with transience and bodiliness and relationship. It is compatible with death on a cross. And so – by extension – it is compatible with a martyrdom like Stephen's, and it is compatible with a call to adventurous discipleship like that Jesus issues in his words 'I am the Way, the Truth and the Life', or in his call 'Follow me!'. Christians are called to follow Jesus as the Israelites once followed the moving pillar, for his embodiment of the *Shechinah* echoes this too: along with Temple and tented tabernacle, it is column of fire and column of smoke. Jesus Christ is 'the vanguard of the redeemed humankind', and our journeying with him is 'the overture of the new creation of all things'. Our being 'in Christ' brings us into 'the moving living space of the coming of God'.[11]

The phrase 'Running to Stand Still' has been made famous in a U2 song. As in that song, it is a phrase that can suggest something of the desperation of human life, where if you stop struggling, even for a moment, you will go backwards, and maybe even fall into catastrophe. Cycling back from my office on the Strand each evening I pass a huge Virgin Active gym full of city workers pouring with sweat on conveyor-belt-like running machines. It's an image for me of the city itself, where everyone must hurry or be left behind. But it's not an attractive image of *home*.

The Gospel of John, meanwhile, gives us a different version of the paradox. It tells is that to abide we must journey; to have truth and life (to have *true life*) we must be always underway. And despite its superficial similarity to the running machine, this message means something quite different. Because neither stasis nor sweaty exhaustion is the result. A life of growth and surprise and relationship and invention and also sometimes (as in Stephen's case) the dramatic transfiguration which is martyrdom – *this* is the nature of the Way which is also Home; the Way in which we are conformed to Christ and embraced by glory.

In the light of this it is perhaps possible to make better sense of the fact that on the one hand Christian people have been called to live lives of abiding, while at the same time they have been told, puzzlingly, that they have no abiding city. They are invited to exchange *changeless abiding* into *changeable abiding*, as Damiel the angel did. The stories of the exodus, the wisdom learnt in exile (to which Jeremiah gives voice), and the vision of the incarnation as Christ moving through the desert with us, all show us something profound about God the Abider.

God's is an abiding that moves. We are often nearest to him when we are moving too. In showing us this truth about God, these texts show us the grain with which we are meant to live, and the joy that can attend a full entry into the world's dizzying, exhilarating flow. They show us that, in Christ, our journey is our abode, and our Way is our Life's Truth. And they point us to the Church; the community that transforms running so as to stand still into travelling so as to abide.

Coda

I want to recall for a second time the question of Psalm 137: 'How could we sing the LORD's song in a foreign land?' Despite the positive things that have been said in this chapter about the way that living 'out of control' can be a form of conformity to Christ (and therefore a deep 'being at home' with God), and despite the optimism I have expressed about the ways that exiles are like guests who can give transformative gifts to their host culture, the fact remains that exile can be hard and miserable. This was the discovery of the Prodigal Son, whose story is told in the excerpt from Luke's Gospel set for the Fourth Sunday in Lent, as he grovelled in the slurry.

Modern Christians live in the market-governed world of global capitalism, and this world is not innately hospitable to religious values, practices and commitments. It can be a hard world for modern Christians to abide in; living in it can feel like a sort of exile.

In the decades since the end of the Second World War the development of the global market has become an overriding economic fact, and the rule of the market means the exhaustive quantification of everything we do. Our activities are, as Nicholas Boyle has pointed out, 'broken down into measurable units, comparable with the units into which the behaviour of others, anywhere in the world, has [also] been broken down'. We are allowed 'no standing in this new world order... that is not transparently related to [our] performance indicator, [our] input-output ratio'. Meanwhile, '[m]ore or less gradually every non-quantifiable... element' finds itself 'leached out of the system of exchange'. A shared day of

161

rest, for example – once valued highly for the solidarity it represented, for being a collective acknowledgement of the Sabbath grace which makes possible all our endeavours – comes to be 'redefined as a free lunch', which must be 'paid for further down the line by somebody else'.[12]

If there were once diverse ways of defining *who we are*, then now those who look for jobs enter a market in which the demand for accountability tries to reduce that diversity to what, following Boyle, we may call:

> [the] uniformity of different calculations
> in the same currency of somebody's
> costed time... The concept of a vocation,
> of a job – or task – for life, that defines
> a large part of what a person is, loses its
> value, and is actively persecuted. We may
> still say 'she is a printer', 'he is a teacher'
> but what we mean, and what in future
> we shall increasingly say, is, 'she is doing
> some printing, at the moment', 'he is on
> a three-year teaching contract'.[13]

Everyone and every activity in our society now finds itself multiplied and precisely quantified and valued: 'productivity, efficiency, performance, cost/benefit..., credit and audience ratings, popularity polls'. There has never been a world order which 'knew so precisely what it valued and how much'. And, as Boyle concludes, it is the market that is now the real repository of value and of truth.[14]

Abject in the pigsty, the lost son reached a point of insight. He realized that this degrading environment could *not* define who he was. In the wonderful words of the parable, *'he came to himself'* (Luke 15.17). His exile became the occasion for his self-discovery.

How can Christians in the modern West 'sing the LORD's song' when the market rules in the way that it does, seeking to exhaustively define exactly who everyone is? There is an irony here, in that *literally* the LORD's song remains quite popular.[15] In some of its forms, religious music is leapt upon as a thoroughly marketable commodity, and the production of best-selling CDs of choral music proves it: the LORD's song is a popular form of 'smooth classic', well-suited to helping the stressed and overworked to 'unwind', and especially enjoyable at Christmas.

But singing the LORD's song means more than making music; it means witnessing that one has a source of identity and meaning that is not dictated by a debased world of values.

So how can we sing what is genuinely the *LORD's* song, and not just a 'smooth classic' that has borrowed its trappings? The lost son in the parable 'came to himself' by recalling the beauty and order of his father's house, as though across a great distance. The memory of it found him out, perhaps a bit like a strain of music, and he responded with his whole being. Maybe the activity of *worship* – and not just of *singing* – is the proper response of Christians to the strains of God's call that they hear as they labour in the assertive and often inhumane market-world. Worship is the response of our whole being to the call of God; it is a repeated 'turning towards home', running towards the embrace of God's welcoming arms. Yes, Church music can be separated from 'Church', and this is generally what happens whenever it is packaged and sold. But worship itself (which is the ultimate context for Christian singing) is different. Worship *cannot* be separated from life in the Church, and it is thereby protected (and capable of protecting *us*) from commodification.

And how can we sing *in a strange land*? Worship, for Christians, can be done anywhere; and it is done – fundamentally – for the good of the whole world and not just of the worshippers themselves. So it is both *resistance* to its environment and *gift* to its environment all at the same time. Singing the LORD's song in a strange land is thus not just something that *can* be done; it is something that *should* be done. God's will to restore people to freedom before him, to overturn the idolatrous service of other gods, needs people who will use their voices to 'sing his new song' – in other words, to worship – to the furthest corners of the earth.

The early Christians may have handled the currency of the Empire each day, but before any of that, before sunrise, they met as the people of God, as the Church. That was their true city, their real 'kingdom', their Jerusalem. Christians' present challenge, too, is to live and work in the world in such a way that the song they sing as people in the Church is strong enough and beautiful enough to relativize and transform other less sacred songs.

By refusing to live by the market's values *alone*, by placing their vocational centre of gravity in another place, in another framework of value, by continuing to assert that there is another song that can be sung, Christians perhaps do more than they imagine to show up the deficiencies of the market's claims – and serve the world better than the market can ever serve it.

6
WOUNDS THAT ABIDE

One of the greatest female saints of the early Church was a woman named Macrina. She lived from around 330 until her death on 19 July, 379 – a death that was recorded lovingly and in considerable detail by one of her brothers, Gregory of Nyssa.

Macrina is evidence that holiness can run in families – or at least that families can be contexts where people educate and encourage one another in holiness. Not only did she and her mother work together to turn their home and estates (in what is now north-eastern Turkey, near the southern coast of the Black Sea) into a flourishing religious community, but her four brothers were all holy men, and two of them – Gregory and Basil – were some of the great bishop-theologians of the Church's history, making up two thirds of that triumvirate later known as the 'Cappadocian Fathers'.

Gregory revered his older sister, as every line of his *Life of Macrina* testifies. She is an inspiration and a model of sanctity for him: he calls her a Mother, Father, Teacher, Tutor, Advice-Giver, all in one. He is ready to use very exalted language about her, describing her life as 'angelic', and calling her 'perfect [...] in every department of virtue'. And, as though her perfection in virtue were finding its natural outward complement, he also describes her exceptional beauty, which was the cause of her being deluged with suitors, all seeking her hand in marriage, before she decided to embrace a celibate life under religious vows. But she emerges as a very human figure, nonetheless. It does not feel as though Gregory has artificially idealized her in a way that makes her difficult to relate to. Rather, it seems that her profound sanctity was grounded in her life, her relationships, and her place – and (as we shall see) in her dying and death.

Gregory found himself present at Macrina's death almost by accident. It was to have a huge impact on him, to which subsequently he clearly wanted to leave a testimony – and this is almost certainly why something like half of the *Life of Macrina* is actually about her death.

He was a hard-pressed bishop in difficult times, and had not had an opportunity to visit his sister for some years, when he found himself travelling within reach of the community where she lived and decided to go to her. It was a journey of several days, and as he drew near he began to have intimations of what he would find on arrival:

> Now when I had accomplished most of
> the journey and was one day's journey
> distant, a vision appeared to me in
> a dream and filled me with anxious
> anticipations of the future. I seemed to
> be carrying martyrs' relics in my hands;
> a light came from them, such as comes
> from a clear mirror when it is put facing
> the sun, so that my eyes were blinded by
> the brilliance of the rays. The same vision
> recurred three times that night. I could
> not clearly understand the riddle of the
> dream, but I saw trouble for my soul,
> and I watched carefully so as to judge the
> vision by events.[1]

He continued on his journey the following day, and was met in advance by a servant, who warned him that his sister was gravely ill. His premonitions of woe continued to grow. When he did at last arrive, he was led to the 'holy dwelling' in

169

which his sister was lying, 'terribly afflicted with weakness'.

> She was lying not on a bed or couch, but on the floor; a sack had been spread on a board, and another board propped up her head, so contrived as to act as a pillow, supporting the sinews of the neck in slanting fashion, and holding up the neck comfortably.

He does not know it yet, but Macrina has only one more night to live, and will die the following day. These precious hours give Gregory the opportunity for a series of intense and moving final conversations with her, in which she recalls the blessings of her life and shares them with him. Then progressively, as the final day of her life slips by, her speech becomes wholly prayer, her prayer (as her voice fails) becomes wholly silent prayer, and finally she passes from this life.

At Macrina's request, Gregory is closely involved in the preparation of her body for burial, as well as with the conduct of her funeral, and it is in the preparation of her body that he encounters a *scar*. It is pointed out to him by the sister of the community who is helping him. She lays bare part of Macrina's chest:

> 'Do not let the great wonders accomplished by the saint pass by unnoticed,' she remarked [...] 'What do you mean?' I said. 'Do you see,' she said, 'this small faint mark below the neck?' It was like a scar made by a small needle. As she spoke she brought the lamp near to the place she was showing me. 'What is there surprising,' I said, 'if the body has been branded with some faint mark in this place?' 'This', she replied, 'has been left on the body as a token of God's powerful help'.

It turns out that Macrina had in earlier times had a life-threatening tumour on that spot, which resulted in an open sore, and which was so near her heart as to make it inoperable.

But she found herself the recipient of a miracle of healing, in which the tears shed during long prayers were mixed with the mud of the sanctuary where she prayed, and this mud – applied to her breast by her mother in the sign of a cross – was followed by an extraordinary recovery.

The story of the miracle itself is remarkable enough, but what is *also* remarkable to Gregory is that the 'tiny trace' he is now looking at was left behind. The healing is not the eradication of all sign that there was ever a tumour there. The skin does not revert to total, unbroken smoothness. A mark on the skin abides, as a sign of what has happened; a witness to the history to which Gregory himself is now witnessing as well.

> '[T]his,' said [the woman], 'is the tiny
> trace of it; it appeared then in place of
> the frightful sore and remained until
> the end, that it might be, as I imagine,
> a memorial of the divine visitation, an
> occasion and reminder of perpetual
> thanksgiving to God.'

What might be learnt from a wound whose scar never fades; a wound whose trace is ordained to 'remain until the end' even though the wound itself is healed?

We live in a world in which it is always possible, or so it seems, to wipe our slates clean. There are more and less trivial examples of this. The rise of the social networking site has given people the opportunity to construct the public persona that they have, with a range of photographs, messages, and links that tell the world what sort of a person they are (or perhaps – more truthfully in many instances – what sort of a person they would *like* to be, or feel they *have* to be).

But social networking sites have also given people the power to revise that persona at will. A 'new you' can be depicted relatively easily. On another scale, it is now common for figures held responsible for organizations or institutions in which there has been some kind of corporate failure to be asked to resign as soon as the scandal comes to light. This may well be an appropriate way of expressing accountability in many cases, and if such figures *never* resigned, and carried on just as before, then there would be something seriously unhealthy about our public life. But to assume that the main two options are only *either* carrying on scot-free *or* walking away can sometimes seem, in a Christian perspective, like a failure of moral imagination.

What about trying to take responsibility for the mess, by staying, but on new terms? A high-profile politician or banker who resigns because something happened on his or her 'watch' will usually pop up in a new and comparable role sometime not long afterwards. It is all very well such people leaving, but when the grand gesture is over, what *abides* (for someone else to sort out) is the set of problems which was the reason for their resignation.

I have mentioned already my own divorce. One of the commonest, and most inappropriate, fantasies that can encourage a married person or a married couple to seek a divorce is that they will have a 'clean slate' afterwards. There is no clean slate. Clearly that is especially true when there are children from the marriage, but even without them the history of the marriage that has ended is still present to and carried by those who were part of it – however much they may seek to erase the outward signs of that past. If there is an honest recognition by those whose marriages do nevertheless end that the clean slate *is* a fantasy, then they will be far readier to look for an abiding of a new kind (an abiding with that past, and – if possible – with the person with whom they shared it) than they would if they thought they were neatly exchanging 'abiding' for 'walking away'.

The new abiding will be radically different; in some cases it will be very practical, in the form of a commitment to remain materially or financially supportive; in some better cases it may involve friendship and continued close cooperation between the former partners (in the task of parenting, for example). But people's history abides with *them* whether or not they want it to, and the best thing to do is search for good ways to abide with *it* in return. Macrina's history continued to abide with her, in the form of the scar above her heart, but also – as her farewell dialogues with Gregory reveal – in her thankful memories of a whole life lived in awareness of and love for God. She did not need to kill her history; she was reconciled with it.

Christianity teaches the possibility of new beginnings. This is at the heart of a Gospel which proclaims not only the power but the *longing* of God to forgive sins and restore life to his people. But new beginnings are not clean slates in every respect. Redeemed human beings will carry with them the marks that show they have a history of sin, and only as such a history of forgiveness; a history of suffering, and only as such a history of healing. That history makes them who they truly are. In having a history *of* sin, redeemed human beings are not of course like Christ, but in having a history *with* sin they are. Christ himself rises from the grave with wounds that Thomas can place his finger inside, and appears in the Book of Revelation as a slain lamb enthroned.

Paul writes in his Letter to the Galatians: 'I carry the marks of Jesus branded on my body' (Galatians 6.17). The identification of Jesus with him is felt by Paul as extraordinarily close, such that his very *body* has become a 'legible' sign of Jesus's work amongst human beings, as Macrina's body was for the amazed Gregory.

This is not just the literal legibility of a written document – the legibility Paul is after in that same epistle when he pushes the scribe to one side and writes with extra large letters in his own hand (Galatians 6.11). It is legibility in terms of human lives and actions; legibility as the concrete expression of Jesus's meaning and work in the persons (and not just the writings) of his followers and witnesses – and embodied now in people like you and me. It might seem rather audacious to suppose that there can be such a close identification between Christians and their

176

Master – but there is no getting away from the sheer force of what the New Testament seems to imply here.

The birth, life and death of Jesus Christ are to find a real, legible witness in the lives of those who proclaim his words and deeds. While Jesus was alive in the world, God's abiding-with-us was visible and tangible in his body – and it made our friendship with God not an abstract idea but a concrete possibility. The Bible tells us that after Jesus's death, resurrection and ascension, the *apostles*, in the power of the Holy Spirit, were able to incarnate the *same* friendship for others: Christ's friendship. Through the Holy Spirit, a real identity could come about between Christ and his witnesses. Hence those words: 'He who listens to you listens to me' (Luke 10.16). Jesus speaks *as* the apostle, *in* the apostle, *in* the person who physically stands there and tries faithfully to say God's word of friendship to the world.

This identity with Christ in word and action is real even to the extent that St Peter – standing with St John before the 'Beautiful Gate' of the Temple (Acts 3.4) – can say to the lame man 'Look at us'. He dares to have faith that Jesus Christ will be readable in him, in his physical presence to the lame man, in his very body.

This is saying something of immense importance about physicality – about bodies themselves – and it is worth pausing to think about the implications of what is being implied here. Bodies, as well as pieces of paper or papyrus, are places where the Word of God can be legible. Paul clearly knew this. What he asks the Galatians to read is not just his letter but his body, which is written on by God. Paul's sufferings (through illness, floggings, wild beasts and the rest) are carried on his body, and they tell what it is to serve Christ. In doing so, they *tell of Christ*. And they do so more clearly (as Paul vigorously points out) than those other markings on the body which are the markings of circumcision.

The free and saving grace of Christ is *not* automatically readable in the marks of circumcision. In what is inscribed on Paul's body, it *can* more readily be discerned, to those whose eyes have been opened by the Spirit. This is so even though the inscriptions tell of pain. For they tell of more than pain. They tell of Paul's love in response to Christ's love; of freedom from the powers of this world; of new creation. In the face of those who continue to find Christ an illegible figure, who have observed Paul's trials and tribulations and have come to the conclusion that such weakness could never minister the saving power of God, they tell of that fact that precisely in weakness and fragility one can be assimilated to Jesus, and embody Jesus's authentic humanity and saving presence for others. 'Carrying in the body the death of Jesus', so Paul writes elsewhere, 'the life of Jesus may also be made visible in our bodies' (2 Corinthians 4.10).

Bodies, then, are legible things, and Christ can be read in them. We know from our own experience how bodies can be maps of who we are, maps that other people can read. We have features that link us to those we are related to. We develop lines when we have laughed a lot or suffered pain. We can have the marks of indulgence about our bodies, or the marks of deprivation. Bodies, Christians believe, are an integral part of the gift God made when he made us *us*. And bodies are places in which Christ takes shape so that others can look at us and read him there.

In our bodies, then, as in our whole lives, we are to try to become readable as those who are

sent by Christ. The first monks of the Christian
Church knew this well. For the early desert
ascetics, the body was not an irrelevant part of the
human person that could somehow be 'put into
brackets'. It was deeply implicated in the transformation of the soul; in being a good witness
to Christ. They spoke of the body as like a field,
given to them by God to cultivate – a place where
they could work and become spiritually rich. Such
an idea stands against all those strategies that seek
to reject or escape the body – seeing it as a prison
of the spirit and an object of loathing – and all
those strategies which pamper the body or make
it the object of fantastical projections.

Hatred of the body and worship of the body are,
after all, two sides of the same coin, because both
fear its mortality. Neither accepts the body's frail
and wonderful reality; one denies its wonder-
fulness, and one denies its frailty. We often
seem to be awash in a sea of fabulous, beautiful
bodies – dripping from advertising hoardings and
magazine pages, and pouring out through TV
screens. They never grow old; they conceal what
huge sums of money are being spent on them
to keep them looking as they do; a whole army
of people services them as part of a booming

industry; and they don't, on the whole, exist to make us feel better, or to encourage us to rejoice in our *own* bodies. Usually they make us feel slightly dissatisfied and incomplete.

And, most important, they are not legible bodies, or at least, their eloquence is in the service of untruth. They do not tell of Christ. The bodies of superheroes and supermodels cannot witness to the self-giving of the crucified one. To reiterate, they refuse the fact that bodies must die – hence the obsessiveness of the *fight* with the body which lies just below the surface of its apparent exaltation. There is a refusal to believe that the fragility and the mortality of our bodies are things we can trust that God intends and will redeem. There is a refusal to believe that carrying Christ in our bodies (his weakness and death in its inseparability from his new life) is the highest form of witness; that it is a sort of truth-telling, and a recognition of the body's real destiny and purpose.

Something about Gregory's descriptions of Macrina is worth coming back to in the light of all that has just been said about wounds that abide – wounds that leave their marks as signs of a real history lived in a real and not a virtual world. Gregory talked about Macrina as exceptionally beautiful, and as angelic, and as 'perfect'. If we had read those words and had never gone on to accompany Gregory in his discovery of the scar, then we might easily have come away from the narrative with a quite idealized *physical* image of what she looked like – an ideal that might have more in common with classical models of unblemished beauty, or their Renaissance revivals, or even modern, airbrushed confections of how bodies should be.

But without appearing to find it at all odd himself, Gregory seems quite able to reconcile the idea of a wounded, frail and dying body with the ideal of a beautiful, angelic and perfect one. In doing so, he manifests an aspect of what we might call 'the Christian difference' – the difference made in history to views that the most beautiful sort of human person is strong, whole and – probably – youthful. There is nothing wrong with youthful beauty, in Gregory's view: Macrina had it. But she achieves a quite different and possibly greater beauty in her dying and death. Christianity redefines beauty, so as to make room for 'wounds' (and, by extension, the marks of age and sacrifice and experience). It relates beauty to an idea of *glory*, which it believes Christ made visible even as he hung on the Cross.

Gregory's thrice-repeated dream on the night before he reached Macrina was of a glorious light that seemed to emanate from the unidentified relics of a martyr. This light was dazzlingly brilliant. In retrospect, it seems clear that the 'relics' he handles in the dream are of a piece with the beloved body he is soon to dress for burial. The dead Macrina too will be radiant – genuinely beautiful – in her scarred holiness. Out of desire for a sort of sober propriety, it is decided to cover her dressed body with one final garment – the dark cloak that was once her mother's. And so, as Gregory recounts:

> [T]he robe was laid upon the body. But
> she was resplendent even in the dark
> robe, divine power having added, as I
> think, this final grace to the body, so that,
> as in the vision of my dream, rays actually
> seemed to shine forth from her beauty.

This miraculous epiphany confirms the meaning of the dream. But far more than that, it confirms a

183

profound Christian commitment to the vulnerable body as a place of glory, because the vulnerable body is the place where Christ is seen and where he makes God known and shareable. Macrina – even in death – proclaims with Paul: 'I carry the marks of Jesus on my body.' Or, to recall the original Greek word: 'I carry the *stigmata* of Jesus on my body.'

The vision of glory that Christians have glimpsed in Christ, and which is fulfilled ultimately ('escha-tologically') in a world transformed, has the effect of redefining how bodies can be beautiful. If human nature's measure of perfection is entirely 'this-worldly', then a shapely, physically intact, healthy self is likely to be the ideal, or at least the *norm* against which other conditions of being human are measured. 'What this "in-tactness" means, though', as Natalie Carnes has pointed out, 'is that the self is bounded, closed, finite':

> It is healthy in a world where all healthy things die. When a world that is closed to eschatological becoming is taken as determinative, the self must terminate.[2]

The Christian vision is of selves that do *not* terminate, but that are growing towards a glory that outstrips their best powers of imagination. This vision is not obsessed with 'intactness'. Intactness corresponds to finitude – that is the irony. However, a body that does not cling to intactness can by virtue of that very fact be open to receive a future which is infinite (and therefore perfect in some *different* sense).

Gregory wrote a great deal besides his *Life of Macrina*, including some extraordinarily beautiful commentaries on the Song of Songs, a text which he loved because it painted a picture of the spiritual journey into God as a journey of intense, marvellous, and never-ending desire. There is always more to enjoy in God. The more you have the more you want, and the more you want the more you can have. He was particularly fascinated by the words of the bride to the bridegroom:

> With great delight I sat in his shadow, and his fruit was sweet to my taste. He brought me to the banqueting house, and his intention towards me was love. Sustain me with raisins, refresh me with apples; for I am faint with love. (Song of Songs 2.4-5)

185

Gregory interprets the final phrase as '*wounded* by love'. The bride in the Song, who in his interpretation stands for himself and for every Christian soul, becomes all at once like his dear sister – the bearer of a wound. This wound ruptures the enclosed human being and sets him in motion towards God, and away from a self-sufficient intactness that will be the inevitable victim of mortality. This is a God-directed openness that will be consummated in eternal life.

And in fact his account of Macrina's death makes just this connection. Macrina, who has, like the bride in the Song, been wounded by love, is as the powers of her body fail her in *full flight* towards God:

> She revealed to the bystanders that
> divine and pure love of the invisible
> bridegroom, which she kept hidden and
> nourished in the secret places of the
> soul, and she published abroad the secret
> disposition of her heart – her hurrying
> towards Him Whom she desired, that she
> might speedily be with Him.

Coda

In the Letter to the Philippians, set as a reading for the Fifth Sunday in Lent, Paul writes:

> For [Christ's] sake I have suffered the loss of all things, and I regard them as rubbish, in order that I may gain Christ. [...] I want to know Christ and the power of his resurrection and the sharing of his sufferings by becoming like him in his death, if somehow I may attain the resurrection from the dead. (Philippians 3.8b, 10-11)

Paul wants his CV to be a curriculum not of his own life but of *Christ's* life, active within him. Indeed, he wants his CV to be a curriculum of both Christ's life and Christ's *death*, for he knows that the life is stronger than the death, but that sharing in Christ's death is the way to know that victory of his life. To put it another way, he is willing to exchange intactness for perfection.

An intact ideal of the body often, it seems to me, goes with an antiseptic ideal of the world. I think that people living in contemporary Western societies live in unprecedentedly antiseptic conditions.

187

By that I do not mean to deny that desperate poverty and squalor still blight the lives of many people, and are a disgrace to the societies that tolerate them. What I mean is that our societies are regulated and standardized and policed against contingency and eccentricity and spontaneity in a way that is astonishingly elaborate and expensive. This vast exercise in social organization is often driven by fear. The fear is ostensibly a fear of things that are sub-standard. But sometimes it simply seems to be a fear of anomalies.

The vast appetite that our modern societies have for fictional worlds (like those of J. K. Rowling) in which there is real danger, dirt and oddity seems to me as though it is a covert – possibly even subliminal – protest against an antiseptic world that eliminates the risk of wounds, and if it cannot eliminate them suppresses them or covers them up.

How might we make our own bodies expressive of Christ? The argument of this chapter has been that the answer lies in a differentiated, untidy and sometimes scarred notion of perfection. The Christian body is *not* the iron body of a Superman, who places his body in a gap in the

188

railway line, on a high bridge, to enable the train full of people that is hurtling towards him to pass over safely. The Christian body is *precisely not* that fantasy kind of body; *not* a body free from illness or injury. It is frail and it suffers. And yet it is *in our bodies* that we achieve amazing things every day, which may indeed make Christ legible.

Even if we do not have those 'marks' of Christ that many people think of when they hear the word *stigmata* (wounds in our hands and our feet), nonetheless other things may well be communicated by our bodies and the way we use them. Such things may mean that (like St Peter) we may be looked at – as Christians most certainly are looked at by others in our curious but uninformed society – and something of Christ may be made visible in us.

We may become better witnesses. For amazing things *really are* achieved every day in our bodies and Christ can be and is glorified in these things. We make relationships with our bodies; we show tenderness with them; we express love and create new life in them through our sexual relationships. We give blood from our bodies, or bone marrow, to save other people's lives, and thus give them years of thought, laughter and relationship.

189

Above all perhaps, as our highest calling, we worship, and we worship bodily. We gather our bodies together and we use them to sing with, to pray with, to exchange signs of peace with, to eat and drink Christ with. Christ has a unique legibility when we gather our bodily selves together in this way – and not just our bodies, of course, but all that we are. The congregation gathered for worship and fellowship becomes a sign of Christ's reconciliation, and the promise of his kingdom. And going out from worship in the power of the Spirit, Christians are abidingly marked people, identified with Christ as his witnesses, as living letters written by his own hand.

7
THE PEACE THAT ABIDES

He is forty-something, he is wearing Bermuda shorts, sandals and a bath robe, and he has popped out to his local supermarket for some milk late one evening in Los Angeles. The supermarket is empty except for the girl at the checkout. The man is wearing sunglasses even though it's dark outside. The small television by the checkout is carrying news of the run up to the first Gulf War in 1990, and George Bush (senior) is giving an interview on the White House lawn, with the spinning rotors of a helicopter behind him. By contrast with his martial words ('This aggression will not stand! This will not stand!'), the man in the bath robe seems – as the script puts it – to be someone in whom *casualness runs deep*.

This is the beginning of Joel and Ethan Coen's *The Big Lebowski* (1998), which is something of a cult movie, and like all cult movies leaves some people cold and others larding their conversation with 'classic' lines from the film. I will try in what follows not to come over too much like one of the latter. But the character we first meet in the suburban supermarket is useful to this chapter because – as the deep, drawling tones of the voiceover put it – he is *not* a 'hero':

> [S]ometimes there's a man – I won't say
> a hee-ro, 'cause what's a hee-ro? – but
> sometimes there's a man [...] who, wal,
> he's the man for his time 'n' place, he fits
> right in there...

The man, whose real name is Jeff Lebowski, is known by all his friends as 'The Dude'. Peering over his sunglasses at the US President on the TV screen, he writes a cheque for the absurdly small sum of 69 cents, in payment for his milk, and shambles off into the eye of a storm.

The series of events that unfolds is so complicated as to defy easy summary (and it certainly, for most of the time, defies the comprehension of The Dude), but is initiated by his being mistaken for another Jeff Lebowski (the 'Big' one of the film's title) – a crooked philanthropist with an estranged, and very strange, daughter (who is a conceptual artist), and a gold-digging, trophy wife (who owes money to a pornographer and hangs out with nihilists). The most complicated issue in The Dude's life until this point has been who will win the bowling league in which he spends most of his spare time playing, along with his two teammates, a bombastic and inept Vietnam veteran, and a mild-mannered, self-effacing ex-surfer. Suddenly, the bowling seems like the most *un*complicated thing in his life. It's a positive refuge.

The Dude, in whom 'casualness runs deep', opens this chapter, because the chapter is about something positive – a gift of God, in fact – that the world's tortured convolutions cannot ultimately displace.

It is striking to me that, on the relatively scarce occasions when the word 'abide' still does make an appearance in modern conversation, it is more often than not in some negative or restrictive sense. So, for example, you might hear a person say that they 'can't abide' another person. Or someone might be told to 'abide by the rules'. People talk about abiding sorrows, regrets, or concerns.

Far less frequently do they talk of good things that abide, or of good sorts of abiding. Which is why one of the statements made very near the end of *The Big Lebowski* seems quite deliberately quirky, and is one of the film's most famous lines: 'The Dude abides'. It is said by The Dude to a mysterious stranger in a white cowboy hat, the source of the drawling voiceover at the beginning of the film, who functions a bit like a divine messenger and knows more than seems humanly possible about the narrative he is telling. The stranger repeats the line, smilingly, and then breaks the boundary between our world and the world of the film by looking up and speaking to us directly through the camera:

> The Dude abides. I don't know about
> you, but I take comfort in that. It's
> good knowing he's out there. The Dude.
> Taking 'er easy for all us sinners.

But what might this enigmatic line be suggesting to the film's audience?

St Augustine of Hippo, in *The City of God*, asserts that there is something profoundly encoded in the universe that is more foundational, more primary, more ultimate than conflict. It is peace. The created world is a fallen world, but the fall has not completely effaced the world's good origins. Mythologies of primal violence or of the eternal conflict of opposed principles are not Christian mythologies. Pagan Rome was wrong to believe them, just as later on Friedrich Nietzsche would be wrong to celebrate the war-like 'superman' (or *Übermensch*) as the ideal human being. Before all violence, lack, or competition, there was (says Augustine) fullness, or plenitude.

This means that it should be possible, from a Christian point of view, to think about differences in the created world without assuming that they have to be *competitive* differences. The ideas of the primacy of peace and of non-competitive difference become the distinctive marks of a Christian vision, over against 'secular' accounts of the fallen world, which take the world's violence as basic and necessary features of it (rather than non-original and contingent; the consequences of the Fall).

The 'virtue' that the *secular* (or *pagan*) picture of the world ends up promoting is heroic. It makes the good life inseparable from a vision of threat, deficiency, and terror – and this is closely related to John Milbank's argument in an essay entitled

'Can Morality be Christian?'.[1] The pagan picture makes virtue complicit with threat, because virtue is defined only by reference to a panoply of danger and violence, which the virtuous person is called to face and overcome. Just as, in William Blake's words 'Mercy could be no more/If there was nobody poor',[2] so knowing what virtue will entail depends upon your being able bravely to confront all kinds of evil.

To be virtuous is to be brave, according to the pagan model. It is, interestingly, to have qualities that Aristotle would instantly recognize as really virtuous qualities – for in Aristotle's world, too, the virtuous person is above all a hero. Battle was in many ways the main test of virtue, and the model of virtue was the soldier. The noblest deaths were those deaths that were met with in battle, seeking to enforce and defend the claims of civic society – of one's city-state. Many civil republicans of the Renaissance and Enlightenment made a similar assumption.

This Milbankian view can be contrasted very interestingly with this, just as it can with Paul Tillich's view in his book *The Courage to Be*. In that book, Tillich chooses *courage* as what we might call the main 'virtue' that he wants to commend to Christians – and he correlates his idea of courage with what Christians have usually called 'faith'. He does this by arguing that courage, like faith, is a sort of affirmation (a self-affirmation, and an affirmation of being). On this basis, Tillich turns to examine 'that against which courage stands'. He has to do so, because courage cannot be understood apart from what it is defined against, and so he talks about the interdependence of courage and anxiety:

> [I]t is necessary for an ontology of courage to include an ontology of anxiety, for they are interdependent.[3]

And he uses revealing terms like '*basic* anxiety',[4] thus signalling a view of anxiety as universally foundational to human existence.

In the terms of Milbank's vision this has the effect of confirming and even promoting a way of life *governed and informed by threat*, and therefore a way of life that is the *opposite* of the life of faith. The figure of Brave Sir Robin, whom we encountered in Chapter 3 of this book, was an example of the problems of just such

197

a threat-governed life, and we contrasted him there with the model of Christian abiding which is that of the shepherd. Like the carer who does not hide behind 'armour', the Christian abider should not need to steel herself in the face of anxiety.

For Milbank, the life of faith stands against reactive and fearful forms of life (of which we might argue, in the end, Tillich's is one). Tillich's model of courageous self-affirmation runs the risk of being *reactive* in character, and of assuming a sort of *scarcity* – that is, the scarcity of meaning and the scarcity of life which are represented by the abyss of meaninglessness and by the apparent ultimacy of death.

Of course, these concerns of Tillich's – which he allows to structure so much of his thought – have to be understood against the background of the deeply nihilistic situation from which that thought emerged (the rise of fascism and the horror of the Second World War). To understand that set of historical circumstances and experiences is to understand a great deal about why someone would want to write a theology of the Christian life like his.

But if Tillich's concerns are a response to one sort of cultural context (Nazism and world war), they go on to feed another one – those of an individualistic, competitive and, yes, *heroic* view of society like that found in a strong tradition of Western, and perhaps especially American thought (the George Bush clip in *The Big Lebowski* proclaims this 'heroic' tradition). A courage-centred theology lends itself to the authentication of such a heroic society, in which the human being turns out to be his or her own saviour, through acts of brave self-affirmation in the face of fear.

'Let the same mind be in you that was in Christ Jesus' (Philippians 2.5). Is Christ's death on the cross a sort of soldierly act – an act of fortitude and self-sacrifice, living out of the evil it opposes? Milbank would answer 'no', and one of the ways in which he sketches an alternative is by looking, in passing, at *hobbits*. Hobbits, of course, are little folk ('halflings'), and they live in a small, friendly corner of what Tolkien calls 'Middle Earth', until a small number of them are caught up into a great battle for the future of their world. The genius of Tolkien's placing of hobbits in the middle of a heroic world is that they stand in contrast to heroes in a fundamental respect. They do not show the sort of courage that is a steely act of will, braced against a threat or evil that has been fully imagined in advance.

They act as they do because they have always lived in an innocent world, in which it is inconceivable to act in any *other* way than they do – with a goodness not calculated, weighed and pitched at some opposing evil, but with a virtue that is part of their habitual being. They have always lived in a world of companionability, firesides, unlocked front doors, trust – a world where there is always enough, and no need to hoard against the threat of scarcity, or to arm against the threat of violence. They have not been trained all their lives in the imagination of danger, as heroes have, and what Milbank calls 'the man of Sparta or Gordonstoun'.[5]

Does this mean that they face danger less well than the hero?

It does not. The heroic man is being determined by dangers all the time – bigger and bigger ones. His whole life is governed by their presence (or even just their imagined presence). The hobbit is shocked by even the smallest acts of violence, and will not – indeed, cannot – be determined by them. Hobbits may not strictly speaking be *sinless*, to use Christian terms, but they are in some way saintly. They have a goodness that is undetermined, unconstrained by evil. In this respect, they are a better place to look than the conventional hero to find out what imitation of Jesus Christ might involve, the Christ who himself lives out the confidence of the original goodness of the world, and the assured goodness of its final end.

In this context – alongside hobbits – we might also think of sheep. As the New Testament writers know, a sheep is a better illustration for what the Christian life involves than a hero. Christians may not feel very flattered by this, but it's true. After all, a sheep lives in trust. It knows and faithfully follows its master, keeping company with others as it does so. And it doesn't spend its time worrying about whether there will be enough grass.

We could say, then, (against Tillich) that imitation of Christ is not for heroes. It is for people who live in the assumption of plenitude. To believe in plenitude is to believe in the already commenced and yet-to-come restoration of all things – and so to live the Christian life means to live in confidence in this fullness – in the necessary, undefeatable goodness that is at the origin of the world (prior to all fear, lack or death) and which will be its fulfilment.

The bowling alley in *The Big Lebowski* – like the Shire in Tolkien's Middle Earth – is the nearest thing in the world of the film to paradise, despite the presence of a slithery opponent to The Dude and his friends who in a touch of surreal irony is named 'Jesus' – a serpent in the garden whose main characteristic is his crazed obsession with competition. In the end, the dominant mark of the bowling alley is that it is a place of friendship. It is not a world not dictated to by lack or fear; it is a world where casualness can run deep.

Now there are of course definite limits to the comparisons that can be made between The Dude and Christ. The Dude is – so the voiceover tells us – 'quite possibly the laziest man in Los Angeles County, which places him high in the running for laziest worldwide'. He is a slob, a drinker, a drug-taker and has causal sex when the opportunity arises. But from the point of view of the Coen brothers, he's something much more than this – even if he doesn't know it. He's a sign of contradiction. He represents another way of being in the world from that which drives the predatory, lying, aggressively self-seeking characters around him. He does not do so because he has a *policy* of contradiction, or a plan of resistance. He is a sign of contradiction because his way of being seems to be rooted in a different sense of his world from those around him.

This also makes him a *judge* – though quite unintentionally. He is not a 'hee-ro'; rather, he just carries on being himself. But the effect of this on the world around him is extraordinary. He becomes an offence and a provocation. The 'principalities and powers' of the world break their cover in the sequence of events that brings The Dude into contact with them – and we see them for what they are: grotesque, vain, greedy, proud, violent.

To reiterate, this does not happen because The Dude is bravely seeking to confront them; he is simply living out of what might be called his 'primal innocence'. He shows up the emptiness of the other Lebowski (the 'Big' Lebowski) and his obsession with presidential connections and civic honour (in which The Dude is *utterly* uninterested). His unheroic series of minor martyrdoms (he is involved in several car crashes, beaten up three times, doped, verbally abused, attacked in his bath, thrown out of a taxi by the irate driver because of a difference in musical taste, and hit in the head by a hurled coffee mug), highlights at different points the brutality of a police chief, the cynicism of a porn magnate, the pretentiousness of the contemporary art world, the rule-bound, self-serving commercialism of the funeral industry, and the moral vacuity of nihilism.

It is, in a surreally comic register, like a separation of the children of light from the children of darkness (1 Thessalonians 5.4-8; 1 John). By comparison with The Dude's basic integrity (even when he is at his most undignified and most incoherent) the 'regular' world looks ludicrous, mad, idolatrous.

I have conceded that laziness is not one of The Dude's Christ-like qualities. But actually, *even in his laziness*, in his ability to be at ease in a world that is paranoid and frantically self-serving, there is something that can echo a religious trust in the deep abiding power of peace.

The story of Jesus's capacity to sleep in the middle of a storm at sea is one of the most vivid moments in the Gospels. Like the moments when we are told that Jesus wept, or was moved to anger, or looked at the rich young man and loved him, all of which have a real, recognizable human naturalness to them, we are told in Mark 4 that Jesus fell asleep.

Sleeping is one of the things that *creatures* do, but which – in traditional ways of thinking – God *doesn't* do. So, for example, right at the beginning of the Book of Genesis – as we are first becoming acquainted with what a human being is in the person of Adam – we see God causing a deep sleep to fall upon him (Genesis 2.21).

Adam sleeps. That's because he's a creature and God made him do it. *God* doesn't need to. Perhaps we remember the great phrase from the Psalms – the one 'who keeps Israel [i.e. God] will neither slumber nor sleep' (Psalm 121.4). So it is an amazing thing, then, to find Jesus, whom Mark's Gospel is proclaiming as the divine Son, *sleeping*. It is an illustration of what God's taking our human nature upon him actually involves.

The particular *circumstances* in which Jesus sleeps here are even more amazing – one might even say, bizarre.

> A great gale arose, and the waves beat
> into the boat, so that the boat was
> already being swamped. But he was in
> the stern, asleep on the cushion; and they
> woke him up and said to him, 'Teacher,
> do you not care that we are perishing?'
> He woke up and rebuked the wind, and
> said to the sea, 'Peace! Be still!' Then the
> wind ceased, and there was a dead calm.
> (Mark 4.37-39)

Jesus sleeps in the middle of a huge storm, whilst the disciples frantically rush around trying to keep afloat. We can be sure that they must have been very frightened indeed to behave like this. They were not novices when it came to boats, and to the behaviour of the weather. They were professionals – or at least several of them were: men who had worked around and on the Sea of Galilee for their whole lives. They were people with real experience and competence. Jesus curiously (on the face of it) was one of the least likely to know what he was doing – he was from Nazareth, much further away from any big stretch of water, and not a fisherman but a carpenter.

On the face of it, perhaps, he didn't appreciate the dangers. He appears to sleep in blissful ignorance – like a child unaware of the fact that his parents' world is falling apart. You can imagine such a situation: a mother being made redundant, or a father being diagnosed with a life-threatening illness, and putting a brave face on it for the children, who sleep an unruffled sleep, while the parents lie awake staring into the darkness, wondering what on earth they are going to do...

Such sleep is the sleep of innocence, like that of Adam in the Garden of Eden – like that deep sleep which the Lord God caused to come upon him, in which he had nothing to fear.[6] There was seemingly no chaos against which frantically to defend himself and safeguard his life. That was humanity's first sleep – the sleep of a child. Adam slept secure in the knowledge that God was providing for him – that his deepest desires were things that God made it his concern to meet (for example in the creation of a companion – Eve – to share his life in the garden).

But what conceivable place can such sleep have in the fallen world we know and into which we have now 'grown up'? Sleep like that has taken on a quality of naivety for us; it has to be paid for by other people's vigilance and work. We have lost our innocence – the innocence of Eden, or the innocence of childhood. And insomnia has become almost the defining affliction of the modern age. It often feels to me as though a great part of the human race now lies awake at night, staring into the dark and wondering what on earth to do, or else for all its competence and technical ability, rushes about frantically trying to keep itself afloat.

The words on millions of lips and passing through millions of minds are the words of the disciples – the words of a lost innocence – 'we are perishing!'. Today's world barely sleeps. If it lets its vigilance slip for a single moment, it fears disaster. Never has there been a world so obsessed with surveillance. We watch the markets every second of every day and night, we put up CCTV cameras in every corner, we have 24-hour news channels and the proliferation of talk, analysis and information, we watch the Middle East; we watch the Chinese; we watch for the enemy within.

Never have we had so much technical ability and power of control. Like the disciples with their boats, we are *competent*. But never have we realized our own fragility so much; never have we had such a sense of lost innocence before; never have we slept so badly.

But Jesus did not sleep because of naivety, however much (superficially) that might seem to be the case. His sleep is not an expression of *casualness*; it is an expression of *peace*. And here, perhaps, we reach the point at which the analogy with *The Big Lebowski*'s loveable Dude reaches its limit: the casualness of The-Dude-who-abides may offer an important corrective to the self-serving, pushy and greedy values that dominate his environment, but there is more to the peace which Jesus models than casualness.

Jesus's sleep was not the thoughtless sleep of one who depends on other people's vigilance and work. Jesus was not under the illusion that he was still in the Garden of Eden. He knew the cost of being part of a desperate, fallen world. Later, in the Garden of Gethsemane, it was precisely *he* who stayed awake while *others* slept – staring into the darkness and wrestling with what it seemed he must do to keep the world afloat.

He stayed awake in order to look open-eyed into the face of the world's fallenness, and to find there a task that only he, the obedient one, could perform – and that he *would* perform on human beings' behalf. He stayed awake, then, in a way that only he could, accommodating his disciples' inability to stay awake with him. He made it possible – in principle – for them to sleep trustfully again. In his faithfulness he opened a way to a new life which gives his followers the blessed assurance that death and chaos will not prevail against it, and that they will not ultimately perish. He restored lost innocence.

So the episode in the storm on the Sea of Galilee can, I suppose, be read as an early sign of that new life to which Jesus has come to open up the way – a sign of what is being restored to human beings in his life, death and resurrection. It shows the second Adam reconstructing and displaying the paradisal blessedness of the first, for the sake of those who are being redeemed. It is a glimpse of the sleep of innocence which is promised to our insomniac age if we will trust

210

the faithfulness of God and follow Christ. Christ stood in our place for us – he stayed awake that we might sleep. But here – in this little excerpt from Mark's Gospel – he also *sleeps* for us. He gives us an example of how we are to sleep, in the light of our redemption. We are to sleep because God is for us, and because God is faithful – the God to whom the earth belongs, and all that is in it, and all who dwell therein. For it is he who founded it upon the seas, and made it firm upon the rivers of the deep (Psalm 24.2). His sleep on the Sea of Galilee is a proclamation of the peace which abides.

'Peace I leave with you; my peace I give to you', says Jesus (John 14.27); and again, 'I have said these things to you so that my joy may be in you, and that your joy may be complete' (John 15.11). Peace, and the joy that follows from it – these are things *promised*. But they are promised because they are *ultimate*. They are not just 'up ahead'; they are the deepest truths of the world, and have been ever since it was made, because they are part of the fullness of God who made the world good. By restoring perfect peace and complete joy to his followers, Jesus restores them to a relationship with their good beginnings as well as their good end, and gives them the ground from which all right agency stems: an assurance that 'aggression will not stand'. Not because of some other and greater aggression, but because the God of peace, who brought again from the dead our great Shepherd of the sheep, is the guarantor of what finally *abides*.

The Greek word *menein* ('abide') is woven through John's Gospel more than any other part of the New Testament – appearing some 40 times in one form or another (and many more times again in the Johannine letters). Its being woven through the text in this way signals the weaving together of other things too: the weaving of people with Christ, Christ with the Holy Spirit, Christ and the Holy Spirit with the Father, and people with one another. This happens in beautifully subtle – almost subliminal – ways in the structuring and phrasing of the Gospel. For example, in John 1.32-33, the Baptist describes a vision in which he sees the Holy Spirit descend from the heavens like a dove and *abide*, or *remain*, on Jesus.

Unlike the public and populated scene of Jesus's baptism as narrated in the synoptic Gospels of

Matthew, Mark and Luke, this vision has an atmosphere of mystical stillness, as though it is an insight into the heart of some timeless truth about Jesus: Jesus dwells in the power of the Spirit, the Spirit dwells on Jesus. It is a vision of profound peace. So when, just a few verses later (John 1.38-39), the two disciples of John the Baptist encounter Jesus and make their first question to him 'where are you abiding?' (using the same verb, *menein*) it is hard not to feel that this is a mystical as well as a practical question. Yes, they want to know where he is lodging (in what building, or in whose house), but whether they know it or not they are also asking a profound question about where Jesus's *eternally*-abiding 'home' is.

Precisely because 'abiding' has already been associated with the Spirit's presence with Jesus, the word cannot but carry some of the same charge in this apparently ordinary question. It is a question that points to the Spirit. No specific house or building is ever mentioned in reply to the question:

> [T]he evangelist leaves it out in order to suggest that, regardless of where Jesus

213

may have been lodged physically, his primary abode was spiritual, or Spirit-related. The Spirit abode on him, the lamb of God, and he, being the lamb of God, abode in the Spirit. It is an intimation of a theme, that of mutual indwelling, which at a later part of the gospel will become more explicit.[7]

So these first two disciples model what should be a primary concern of any follower of Christ – to seek out the deep mystery of the source of his being: his life in and as God. The eternal place of Jesus's abiding is what those who follow him are *meant* to look for. That in turn makes Jesus's next words to the enquirers a cause for wonder and joy. He says: 'Come and see', and they are permitted to 'remain with him' (again, the verb *menein*). They, too, now 'abide'. First the Spirit, then Christ, and now the disciples are the subjects of this verb. It extends, like the cloud of glory on the mount of the transfiguration (Luke 9.28-36), to include them too. They become participants in the divine activity of abiding. They dwell in and with God.

Another delicate piece of literary structuring links that call to the first two disciples in the

opening chapter of John's Gospel with the
figure of John the Beloved Disciple in the final
chapter, and again the link is achieved through
the use of the word *menein*. We are told that
one of those first two disciples to have been
called was Andrew, who would go on to bring
his brother Simon to meet Jesus, but the other
is not named; and if, as has been argued, the
anonymous one of those first two disciples was
John,[8] then he becomes, so to speak, the 'first
and last disciple'.

He becomes the Gospel's great *abider*. He *abides*
with Jesus from the very beginning of his ministry
(as a forerunner of Simon Peter himself) until the
very end (for when Simon Peter learns from the
risen Jesus about his own coming death in the
closing verses of the Gospel, he is told that John
will continue to 'remain' or *abide*):

Peter turned and saw the disciple whom
Jesus loved following them; he was the
one who had reclined next to Jesus at the
supper and had said, 'Lord, who is it that
is going to betray you?' When Peter saw
him, he said to Jesus, 'Lord, what about
him?' Jesus said to him, 'If it is my will

> that he remain until I come, what is that
> to you? Follow me!' (John 21.20-22)

This disciple 'whom Jesus loved' is the one whose witness to Jesus is being recorded in the Fourth Gospel. And Jesus indicates that his activity of bearing Gospel witness will abide, 'even after Peter's discipleship has been completed in death',[9] and even after he too has died. His Gospel – a witness to the whole story of Jesus from beginning to end (and from mundane surface to mystical depths) – will *remain* until Jesus comes again.

In all of these contexts, and reaching a high point in the Farewell Discourses of Jesus (especially John 14, 15, and 16), there is in John's Gospel a very special theological usage of the idea of abiding. It informs all the other uses in the Gospel, and it grounds the human abiding of the first disciples with Jesus, as well as the abiding of the Spirit on Jesus in his earthly ministry, in something to do with the life of God the Trinity in its *eternal* character. It is a word that describes the way that God is in God's deepest being – the way that God exists as Father, Son and Holy Spirit.

The unity of God is not a sort of structural fact; it is an *activity* springing from love and faithfulness. Father, Son and Holy Spirit are 'in' one another; being and abiding become, as it were, synonymous. God's being is an 'abiding-being', a mutual indwelling, infinitely intense, infinitely enduring, infinitely peaceable, infinitely joyful. Chapter 15 in particular is a great crescendo of abiding language. But it has at its heart the image of the relationship of *a vine to its branches*, and this is an image which perhaps more vividly than any other extends the 'abiding-being' of Godself to embrace and include human beings too.

A close look at the Johannine use of *menein* shows an extraordinary mutuality in the abiding of God and believers with one another. At various points it is said that the believer abides in God, in Christ, in God's word, in love, in the light. Conversely, it is said that God, Christ, and the Spirit abide in the believer – along with God's anointing, seed, love, and eternal life. In other words, as well as doing his or her own abiding, the believer will also be a place in which abiding takes place. Or to put it another way, God and the believer *both* get to be an 'abode' for the other.

217

This extraordinary mutuality is not totally symmetrical, however. God may make 'life' dwell in the believer, but this does not happen in reverse; the believer does not give life to God. Moreover, the love and the life that make their abode in the believer – while they are really the believer's – do not thereby become the *property* of the believer. Here the image of the vine branch becomes especially helpful: the life of the branch is genuinely its life, but only because it is *also* and *more ultimately* the life of the vine in which the branch abides. The vine's life does not depend upon any particular branch's participation in it, but any particular branch's ability to participate does depend on the vine's life.

Whenever the life of the vine abides in the branch, it is only because the branch abides in the life of the vine. Likewise, God's love and life abide in the believer only insofar as the believer abides in God – the Christian's abiding in God is like being 'plugged into the mains' of eternal life, to use a more modern and rather less beautiful image. As Rudolf Bultmann put it, this sort of abiding is 'loyal steadfastness to the cause only in the sense of always allowing oneself to be encompassed, of allowing oneself to receive'.

> The loyalty that is demanded is not primarily a continued being *for*, but a being *from*; it is not the holding of a position, but an allowing oneself to be held [...][10]

For all its asymmetry, however, the fact remains that the vine image discloses a real and wonderful possibility of participation by creatures in the life which courses through God. Creatures can live not just *in relation to* but *in* God's abiding, as *outgrowths* of it. The abiding into which Jesus gives an insight in his dealings with all those to whom he ministers – and in which he invites his followers to share – is an expression or outflow of *God's own* ('inner') abiding. In the light of this disclosure, the overtones of commitment and solidarity in the relations between creatures that are implicit in the word abiding are immeasurably deepened.

We suddenly understand – for instance – just how *godly* the Good Shepherd's example really was, when we met it earlier in the Gospel. He translates something that originates in God's goodness and life into a very practical, earthly situation: the activity of caring for the vulnerable.

219

He gives to the sheep the very same love and
faithfulness that is, so to speak, God's own 'life
blood'. He doesn't just 'stick around' the sheep;
he is prepared to make the ultimate sacrifice for
them, in order that none of them is lost. His own
self is the guarantee. There is no guarantee more
generous.

Likewise, in being united with Jesus, his disciples
are invited to abide *as God abides in Godself.* They
are called to be imitators of Jesus, whose life is the
perfect expression of God's 'abiding-being':

> Abide in me as I abide in you. [...] As
> the Father has loved me, so I have loved
> you; abide in my love. If you keep my
> commandments, you will abide in my
> love, just as I have kept my Father's
> commandments and abide in his love.
> (John 15.4a, 9-10)

The crucial thing here is that even when there
are sacrificial dimensions to this abiding (as when
the Good Shepherd lays down his life), it is not
anxiety-driven struggle. It is informed not by a
sense of ultimate lack or intense threat, but by a
deep grounding in the fundamental fullness and

the profound and inalienable goodness that are part of God's gift to the world in creating it. It has something like Augustine's vision of plenitude at its heart – a vision we can recognize in the world of the hobbits' Shire or The Dude's bowling alley. To act in contradiction of this vision when 'wolves' come to the door, by mirroring their predation, would be to lose one's very self: to betray everything that made one's life make sense in the first place.

Such a vision is informed by the knowledge that God is love, and that the world lives in God, and that to live violently or fearfully (and the two often go hand in hand) is to live against the grain of the universe – or like a vine-branch apart from the vine. On the occasions when sacrifice in the face of sin and evil is necessary, it will simply be the outflowing of life lived from an assurance of the primacy of peace and of joy – a peace and joy that abide. It is the work not of 'hee-roes' but of saints.

Coda

In the long Gospel reading set for Passion Sunday, Jesus is brought before Pilate and before Herod and before Pilate again, and their self-serving love of power 'breaks cover' when faced with this sign of contradiction: a man who will not answer their questions in the terms they expect and demand. In trying to hound out of him the truth of who *he* is, their 'who?' question rebounds upon them and *their* truth is exposed instead. It is the truth of their sin – and ironically the fact that they *share* it becomes the occasion for a bond between them. As Luke's Gospel tells us, the two men draw closer as a consequence of this encounter with Jesus. 'That same day Herod and Pilate became friends with each other' (Luke 23.12).

The children of darkness are being separated from the children of light. It may seem as though these men of power hold the whip hand, but this is the hour of judgement on *them* (John 12.31).

Jesus's path – echoing that of the Suffering Servant in Isaiah – will now involve sacrifice:

> I gave my back to those who struck me,
> and my cheeks to those who pulled out
> the beard; I did not hide my face from
> insult and spitting. (Isaiah 50.6)

But the readiness to make this sacrifice is grounded in a deeper assurance that violence will not have the last word; that sacrifice is not the abiding order of things, but is instead the side effect of peace's reassertion of its claims in the midst of a fallen world. Pilate's and Herod's aggression 'will not stand' – not because a bigger and more powerful divine aggression is just around the corner to put a stop to them, but because a bigger and more powerful peace is at work in their midst:

> [O]ne of them struck the slave of the high
> priest and cut off his right ear. But Jesus
> said, 'No more of this!' And he touched
> his ear and healed him. (Luke 22.50-51)

Reproduced on the cover of the book is a 1989 work by the English painter Norman Adams (1927–2005), which is called *Christ's Cross and Adam's Tree*. Like so many of Adams's religious paintings, there is a simultaneity of suffering and glory in the image, but the glory is in the ascendant. The cross on which Christ hangs – so often described as a 'tree' – is at the same time the untrumpable declaration of a love and a life that abide – of a God who will absolutely not go away and leave his people comfortless.

Norman Adams's bright colours, and elemental shapes suggest the resurrection breaking through the veil of pain, announcing that even the tree of shame has its roots in the eternal abiding of God's own life; that this life courses through its veins and will make it a fruitful tree. As if to confirm this, meadow flowers seem to spring up around it.

In its own way, this image, too, shows the primacy of peace. Adam's tree sprang up in Eden. When that tree became the source of a fall into a violent order, a second 'tree' was planted to restore the paradise that had been lost. In some legends, the cross was made from the same wood as the tree from which Adam ate, and was planted in the same place.

Here is one last thought, which might yield something to meditate upon in the approach to Holy Week, especially as we consider our homes and those with whom we share them. The painting shows the ultimate abiding of God with us: an abiding in and through death. But it also shows a new human 'abode' being shaped, which is an outflowing of God's transformative abiding in Christ. We are pointed to this human abode in the figures at the foot of the cross – and particularly in the presence there of John and Jesus's mother. This is because in his dying, Jesus bestows them on one another, and enjoins them to abide with one another. His abiding has been the example and is now the well-spring of the abiding they are to do with one another:

> When Jesus saw his mother and the
> disciple whom he loved standing beside
> her, he said to his mother, 'Woman, here
> is your son.' Then he said to the disciple,
> 'Here is your mother.' And from that
> hour the disciple took her into his own
> home. (John 19, 26-27)

This is the tree of the cross already fruiting. A new human abiding is its fruit. Can we bring forth the fruit of the cross in our 'abodes', and make the places where we dwell witness to the firstness and the lastness of peace?

EPILOGUE: WHO MAY ABIDE?

O Lord, who may abide in your tent?
Who may dwell on your holy hill? Those
who walk blamelessly, and do what is
right, and speak the truth from their
heart. (Psalm 15.1-2)

Many people over the centuries have tried to imagine what heaven is like – preachers, poets, painters among them. Moreover, many people have wondered who gets to go there. As the wisest have known, there are limits to how far one can get with such questions and imaginings. Nevertheless, Christians reading texts like the one above, from the Psalms,[1] have been confident that Jesus Christ is one who has walked blamelessly. And they have been joyful in the belief that he offers to share the benefits of this blamelessness, which gives all people the possibility of abiding with him in God's heavenly tent. We may only have indistinct intimations of what heaven is like, but as a consequence of Christ's uniting himself with the human condition, and going before us into new and risen life through the waters of death, all people can hope for a welcome there.

But another question haunts the modern mind, and that is not so much whether I or those with whom I share my life will have a place in heaven, but whether there are 'whos' in heaven *at all*. Does the very fact of being a 'who' – of being a someone, a unique, particular person – mean anything after we die, except in the minds of those left behind?

I was surprised by a recent conversation with a church-going friend who said that she did not expect in any way still to be 'her' after she died. She imagined herself returning to the ebb and flow of the cosmos. And this expectation may be a very widespread one in the popular imagination. An eloquent account of it (which is also a piece of propaganda for it) is found in the final volume of Philip Pullman's trilogy *His Dark Materials*, when the children Lyra and Will travel to the land of the dead, to release a numberless host of whispering shadows from perpetual darkness into a reunification with the vibrant cycles of material life. This release is, of course, a release into 'oblivion', in the sense that all personal consciousness comes to an end, but it is at least a form of living:

> [A] voice cried out, as loudly as a whisper could cry. It was the ghost of a thin man

with an angry, passionate face, and he cried:

"What will happen? When we leave the world of the dead, will we live again?" [...][Lyra] took out the golden instrument. The answer came at once. She put it away and stood up.

"This is what'll happen," she said, "and it's true, perfectly true. When you go out of here, all the particles that make you up will loosen and float apart [...]. If you've seen people dying, you know what that looks like. But [now] they're part of everything. All the atoms that were them, they've gone into the air and the wind and the trees and the earth and all the living things. They'll never vanish. They're just part of everything. And that's exactly what'll happen to you, I swear to you, I promise on my honour. You'll drift apart, it's true, but you'll be out in the open, part of everything alive again."

This is the beginning of a concerted attempt by Philip Pullman to capture the imagination of his readers for a post-Christian vision of death.

The Christian vision is renarrated as a false comfort and a lie, based on a theory that people's eternal destiny will reward them for the way they conducted themselves in this life. His own more materialist vision commends itself by contrast as more *honest* because it is not based on wish-fulfilment (the fantasy that our personal identity can survive death and be rewarded), and as more *attractive* because more beautiful (he pulls out all the stops of his considerable literary powers to evoke the wonder of the universe we are part of, by contrast with the rather abstract, boring-sounding picture of a Christian heaven, which – he seems to imply – is not unlike one long church service). We readers whose imagination he is trying to capture are invited to stand listening to Lyra as the host of the dead listen to her – and we are then given a model of how to respond in the form of a young woman who steps forward to speak:

> She had died as a martyr centuries before. She looked around and said:
> "When we were alive, they told us that when we died we'd go to heaven. And they said that heaven was a place of joy and glory and we would spend

eternity in the company of saints and
angels praising the Almighty, in a state
of bliss. That's what they said. And that's
what led some of us to give our lives, and
others to spend years in solitary prayer,
while all the joy of life was going to waste
around us, and we never knew.

"Because the land of the dead isn't a
place of reward or a place of punishment.
It's a place of nothing. The good come
here as well as the wicked, and all of us
languish in this gloom for ever, with no
hope of freedom, or joy, or sleep or rest
or peace.

"But now this child has come offering
us a way out and I'm going to follow
her. Even if it means oblivion, friends, I'll
welcome it, because it won't be nothing,
we'll be alive again in a thousand blades
of grass, and a million leaves, we'll be
falling in the raindrops and blowing in
the fresh breeze, we'll be glittering in the
dew under the stars and the moon out
there in the physical world which is our
true home and always was.

"So I urge you: come with the child
out to the sky!"[2]

Philip Pullman does Christians a service by reminding them of a thoroughly native tradition of their own – the tradition of celebrating the material creation and not letting the joy of life go to waste around them. (Almost anything written by the great seventeenth-century writer Thomas Traherne could stand as an example of just how Christian a tradition this is.) Pullman also provides a useful warning to those strands of Christian theology which have reduced the wonder of the vision of heaven by over-specifying it.

But there is a sleight of hand in his counter-imaginary exercise. His attempt to make his own vision more beautiful than the Christian one opens him to the accusation that he, too, is involved in an exercise in wish-fulfilment. For his vision of a return to cosmic matter is offered wholly in terms geared to please the human appetite: sweet soil, sparkling stars, champagne bubbles, fresh breezes, glittering dew.

This is a world without bacteria or dirt. And it is a vision which still subtly suggests that we are going somehow to be able to enjoy it, to *prefer* it over the 'nothingness' of the land of the dead.

So, ironically perhaps, Pullman himself cannot entirely break free of two of the cornerstones of a Christian vision of heaven: the idea that *some sort of 'who'* is being satisfied in death, and the idea that this 'who' – of whatever sort – is precisely *being satisfied* in death.

But why regard a vision in which wishes are fulfilled as necessarily a bad thing, anyway? And why assume such wishes can go only so far and no further without tipping into intellectual dishonesty? In projecting what happens to us in death, why be prepared to celebrate our love of sweet earth and starlight, but remain so fiercely suspicious of any intimation of a heaven in which all that we love becomes yet more wonderful, and yet more fully ours? Why automatically assume that a vision in which human desire is satisfied is likely to be less truthful than one in which it is not? What if ultimate truth and personal (which is also social) joy are coincident with one another? Not just in the brief momentary bliss of personal disintegration and reunion with Mother Nature, but in an abiding way that transforms us endlessly and utterly and ecstatically?

This was the hope of Macrina, whose story was traced in an earlier chapter. Pullman may have had people like her in mind when he invented his young woman in the realm of the dead, who finds herself longing for her particles to separate as she heads for the sky.

But Macrina's hope has a rich texture of great beauty, which is not world-denying, and not pettily self-seeking, and above all not *fearful*. Her vision of heaven is of a place of mystical refreshment, and heightened relationship with a God who knows and loves her. This is evident in the words of her final prayer:

> 'Thou, O Lord, hast freed us from the
> fear of death. Thou hast made the end
> of this life the beginning to us of true
> life. Thou for a season restest our bodies
> in sleep and awakest them again at the
> last trump. Thou givest our earth, which
> Thou hast fashioned with Thy hands,
> to the earth to keep in safety. One day
> Thou wilt take again what Thou hast
> given, transfiguring with immortality
> and grace our mortal and unsightly
> remains. Thou hast saved us from the
> curse and from sin, having become both
> for our sakes. Thou hast broken the

heads of the dragon who had seized us
with his jaws, in the yawning gulf of
disobedience. Thou hast shown us the
way of resurrection, having broken the
gates of hell, and brought to nought
him who had the power of death – the
devil. Thou hast given a sign to those
that fear Thee in the symbol of the Holy
Cross, to destroy the adversary and save
our life. O God eternal, to Whom I
have been attached from my mother's
womb, Whom my soul has loved with all
its strength, to Whom I have dedicated
both my flesh and my soul from my
youth up until now – do Thou give
me an angel of light to conduct me to
the placc of refreshment, where is the
water of rest, in the bosom of the holy
Fathers.'

Gregory goes on to describe the quiet assurance
with which she prays herself into death. The
movement is one of 'inward desire', and the faith
that – in a good universe – where there is desire
one can honestly expect to find its fulfilment is
a faith that is palpably present both in Macrina
herself and in those around her:

Meanwhile evening had come and a lamp
was brought in. All at once she opened
the orb of her eyes and looked towards
the light, clearly wanting to repeat the
thanksgiving sung at the Lighting of
the Lamps. But her voice failed and she
fulfilled her intention in the heart and by
moving her hands, while her lips stirred
in sympathy with her inward desire. But
when she had finished the thanksgiving,
and her hand brought to her face to
make the sign had signified the end
of the prayer, she drew a great deep
breath and closed her life and her prayer
together.[3]

On what grounds can Christians sustain their hope
for a heavenly abiding, in which the particular
'whos' that people are will find themselves
safeguarded and treasured?

We can turn for the last time to John's Gospel,
and to the word *menein* ('abide'), to find a
possible answer.

In my Father's house there are many
dwelling-places. If it were not so, would I

have told you that I go to prepare a place
for you? (John 14.2)

The Greek word translated here as 'dwelling-
places' is the noun-form, *mona*, of the verb
menein: it translates as an abode, a dwelling-
place, or (in the unusual Latinate word used in
the King James Bible), a 'mansion'.

'In my Father's house there are many mansions.'
John Ruskin (1819–1900), that most eminent of
Victorians, found himself fascinated by this little
verse, and saw dangers in it for a very contemporary sort of wish-fulfilment:

> Not but that 'mansion' is a very fine
> Latin word, and perfectly correct, (if only
> one knows Latin,) but I doubt not that
> most parish children understand by it, if
> anything, a splendid house with two wings,
> and an acre or two of offices, in the middle
> of a celestial park; and suppose that some
> day or other they are all of them to live in
> such, as well as the Squire's children...[4]

This gives him an occasion to call (in what is
perhaps a somewhat unrealistic hope) for a new

translation in which all the times that the word *menein* and its derivatives appear, they are kept in *Greek* so that the sheer range of use and the theological force of this 'abide' word can be more easily seen:

> If ever your clergy mean really to help
> you to read your Bible, – the whole of
> it, and not merely the bits which tell you
> that you are miserable sinners, and that
> you needn't mind, – they must make a
> translation retaining as many as possible
> of the words in their Greek form, which
> you may easily learn, and yet which
> will be quit of the danger of becoming
> debased by any vulgar English use. So
> also, the same word must always be given
> when it *is* the same; and not in one place
> translated 'mansion,' and in another
> 'abode.' […]

It's an intention with which in its own way this present book has been in sympathy. Start looking for 'abiding' in the Bible and you will find it everywhere, a network of images centred on this one great word, spread through Scripture like a textual correlate to the everlasting arms of God.

The most powerful thing about John 14.2 for the theme of this epilogue, however, is simply the fact that it is in the plural. 'In my father's house there are many *abodes*.' This seems to be a promise that the plurality, the diversity, all the wonderful particularity of persons is meaningfully preserved in heaven. The promise is not of one great big space into which each history, each world of meaning, each face is dispersed. It is a promise of 'differentiated glory', in which there are *many* places of rest for *many* beloved persons.

Just what these will be like cannot responsibly be described or specified, but perhaps one key image – which is another of John's gifts to his readers – is that of the Beloved Disciple reclining at the Last Supper and resting his head on Jesus's side. He has an abiding place in this closest intimacy with Jesus. Just as in the opening call narratives it is as though the first disciples are invited into the abiding that the Spirit and the Son do with one another, so here John has been invited into a divine abiding – this time, like the abiding that the Son does when he dwells in the bosom of the Father.

Jesus abides in the closest intimacy with his heavenly Father; John dwells in the closest intimacy with Jesus. And the appearance of that plural in John 14.2 signals the resurrection hope that is proclaimed every Easter by the Church: in heaven there will be a *multiplication* of this dwelling, '*many dwelling-places*', many Beloved Disciples.[5]

'Who may abide?' Or, to ask the even more basic question, 'may whos abide?' At its best, Christianity finds itself not so much fulfilling a self-interested dream in its belief that 'whos' *do* abide beyond death, as being compelled, in wonder, and as a grace exceeding all expectation, to take this possibility seriously because of what happened to Jesus Christ. He was raised from the dead, he came again and spoke words of love and promise to his followers, he looked into their faces again and let them look into his, and he has gone, as he put it, 'to prepare a place' for those whom he has united to himself.

NOTES

Introduction

1   Another word with negative connotations that suggest a *bad* abiding is 'dallying'. Interestingly, 'dallying' is like 'abiding' in being a word with limited modern usage.

2   This is the title of a major recent work of theological anthropology by the North American theologian David H. Kelsey: *Eccentric Existence: A Theological Anthropology* (2 vols; Louisville, KY: Westminster John Knox Press, 2009).

3   George Eliot, letter to Frederic Harrison, quoted in E. S. Shaffer, *"Kubla Khan" and* The Fall of Jerusalem: *The Mythological School in Biblical Criticism and Secular Literature 1770–1880* (Cambridge: Cambridge University Press, 1975), 228–9.

4   Dietrich Bonhoeffer, 'The Friend' in *Letters and Papers from Prison* (*Dietrich Bonhoeffer Works*, Volume 8), edited by John W. de Gruchy (Minneapolis, MN: Fortress, 2010), 527.

Chapter One

1   Michael Paternoster, *Counsels for all Christians: Obedience, Stability and Conversion in the Rule of St Benedict* (Fairacres: SLG Press, 1980), 1.

2   *The Rule of Saint Benedict*, edited and translated by Bruce L. Venarde (Cambridge, MA: Harvard University Press, 2011), 7–9.

3   *Rule* 2011, 19.

4   Paternoster 1980, 7.

5 *Mission-shaped Church: Church Planting and Fresh Expressions of Church in a Changing Context* (London: Church House Publishing, 2004).

6 Andrew Davison and Alison Milbank, *For the Parish: A Critique of Fresh Expressions* (London: SCM, 2010), xi.

7 Davison and Milbank 2010, 9–10.

8 Davison and Milbank 2010, 92.

9 Davison and Milbank 2010, 63; they are quoting John Milbank, *The Suspended Middle: Henri de Lubac and the Debate Concerning the Supernatural* (London: SCM, 2005), 2.

10 Henry M. R. E. Mayr-Harting, *The Venerable Bede, the Rule of St Benedict, and Social Class* (Jarrow Lecture, 1976), 14; my emphasis.

11 *Rule* 2011, 187–9.

12 Monica Furlong, *Travelling In* (London: Hodder and Stoughton, 1971), 98; cf. Paternoster 1980, 11.

13 John R. H. Moorman, *A History of the Church in England*, 3rd edn (London: Adam and Charles Black, 1973), 44; cited in Robert Hale OSB, 'The Benedictine Spirit in Anglicanism' in *Christian* 5:3 (1980), 40.

14 Peter F. Anson, *The Call of the Cloister: Religious Communities and Kindred Bodies in the Anglican Communion*, revised and edited by A. W. Campbell (London: SPCK, 1958).

15 Cyprian, 'On the Advantage of Patience' in *The Ante-Nicene Fathers*, Volume 5, translated by Robert Ernest Wallis, http://en.wikisource.org/wiki/Ante-Nicene_Fathers/Volume_V/Cyprian/The_Treatises_of_Cyprian/On_the_Advantage_of_Patience, accessed April 2012.

16 *Rule* 2011, 5–7.

Chapter Two

1 Michael Ende, *Momo* (Stuttgart: Thienemann, 1973). I have made my own translations from the book, but there is also a published translation by J. Maxwell Brownjohn (London: Puffin Books (Penguin), 1985). I am grateful to Susanne Prankel for introducing me to Momo.

2 Geoffrey Hill, 'What Devil Has Got Into John Ransom?' in *The Lords of Limit: Essays on Literature and Ideas* (New York, NY: Oxford University Press, 1984), 128–9; he is himself borrowing the phrase from John Crowe Ransom.

3 Simone Weil, *Waiting for God*, translated by Emma Craufurd (New York, NY: Harper and Row, 1951).

4 Luke Timothy Johnson, 'Imagining the World Scripture Imagines' in *Modern Theology* 14:2 (1998), 174.

5 M. Avot 5:26.

6 Fr Luke Dysinger, OSB, 'Accepting the Embrace of God: The Ancient Art of *Lectio Divina*', http://www.valyermo.com/ld-art.html (1990), accessed April 2012.

7 http://www.moma.org/interactives/exhibitions/2010/marinaabramovic/index.html.

8 Jean-Luc Marion, 'Evidence and Bedazzlement' in *Prolegomena to Charity* (New York, NY: Fordham University Press, 2002), 67.

9 Hannibal Hamlin, 'Bunyan's Biblical Progresses' in *The King James Bible after 400 Years: Literary, Linguistic, and Cultural Influences*, edited by Hannibal Hamlin and Norman W. Jones (Cambridge: Cambridge University Press, 2010), 203.

10 Cited in Hamlin 2010, 206.

11 Walker Percy, 'The Loss of the Creature' in *The Message in the Bottle: How Queer Man Is, How*

Queer Language Is, and What One Has to Do With the Other (New York, NY: Farrar, Straus and Giroux, 1975), 47; cited in David H. Kelsey, *Eccentric Existence: A Theological Anthropology* (2 vols; Louisville, KY: Westminster John Knox Press, 2009), 346–7.

12 Roger Fry, *Vision and Design*, edited by J. B. Bullen (Oxford: Oxford University Press, 1981), 33–8.

13 Henry Vaughan, 'The Search' in *The Complete Poems*, edited by Alan Rudrum (Harmondsworth: Penguin, 1983), 157–9.

14 http://www.nationalgallery.org.uk/paintings/ fra-filippo-lippi-the-annunciation, accessed April 2012.

15 John Drury, *Painting the Word: Christian Pictures and their Meanings* (New Haven and London in association with the National Gallery, London: Yale University Press, 1999), 52–3.

Chapter Three

1 A version of Sam Well's typology can be found in his paper 'The Nazareth Manifesto' at http:// www.duke.edu/web/kenanethics/OccPapers/ NazarethManifesto_SamWells.pdf (2008), and another at http://www.westcott.cam.ac.uk/about/ news/Enjoying_God_(2)_Mission_Sept_08.pdf, accessed April 2012.

2 Rowan Williams, *On Christian Theology* (Oxford: Blackwell, 2000), 12.

3 Wells 2008, 4.

4 Wells 2008, 6.

5 Nicholas Adams discusses the role of argument in theology in his chapter 'Argument' in *Fields of Faith: Theology and Religious Studies for the Twenty-First*

Century, edited by David F. Ford, Ben Quash and Janet Martin Soskice (Cambridge: Cambridge University Press, 2005), 137–51.

6 Augustine, *Quaestiones Evangeliorum* (*Questions on the Gospels*) 2.19.

7 We first encountered the Pelagian heresy in Chapter 1, 17.

8 Augustine's views on this topic can be found in his treatise *On Nature and Grace*; see especially, for example Chapter 21: http://www.newadvent.org/fathers/1503.htm, accessed April 2012.

9 Jean Vanier, *Drawn into the Mystery of Jesus through the Gospel of John* (London: DLT, 2004), 260.

10 John Inge outlines this distinction elegantly in his book *A Christian Theology of Place* (Farnham: Ashgate, 2003), 1–2.

11 Sheila Cassidy, *Sharing the Darkness: The Spirituality of Caring* (London: DLT, 1988), 61–3.

12 I am grateful to Eve Poole for this helpful insight.

Chapter Four

1 Ian McEwan, *Enduring Love* (London: Vintage, 1998), 2, 10–16.

2 I owe this phrase and many valuable discussions around the theme to Timothy Jenkins.

3 'The Marriage Service' in *Common Worship* (© The Archbishops' Council of the Church of England), http://www.churchofengland.org/prayer-worship/worship/texts/pastoral/marriage/marriage.aspx, accessed April 2012.

4 '[L]ove is not love
Which alters when it alteration finds,
Or bends with the remover to remove.
Oh no! it is an ever-fixèd mark

That looks on tempests and is never shaken;
It is the star to every wandering bark,
Whose worth's unknown although his height be
taken.
Love's not Time's fool, though rosy lips and cheeks
Within his bending sickle's compass come;
Love alters not with his brief hours and weeks,
But bears it out even to the edge of doom.'
William Shakespeare, 'Sonnet 116' in *Sixty-Five Sonnets of Shakespeare*, edited by W. G. Ingram and Theodore Redpath (London: University of London Press, 1967), 11.2–12. My thanks to Ed and Giulia Barnett whose wedding, and choice of readings, set these thoughts in train.

5 Sonnet 116, 1.6.

6 David H. Kelsey, *Eccentric Existence: A Theological Anthropology* (2 vols; Louisville KY: Westminster John Knox Press, 2009), 427–8. Kelsey is drawing heavily on the work of Rowan Williams in this passage, and in particular Williams's essay 'On Being Creatures' in *On Christian Theology* (Oxford: Blackwell, 2000), 63–78.

7 David F. Ford, *The Shape of Living* (London: HarperCollins, 1997).

8 Thomas Aquinas, *Summa Theologica* Ia, Question 93, Article 3; cf. http://www.ccel.org/ccel/aquinas/summa.toc.html, accessed April 2012.

9 Shawn Reeves, 'Who's More Like God – Angels or Humans?', http://www.catholicillini.com/2010_09_01_archive.html, accessed April 2012.

10 Reeves, 2010.

Chapter Five

1 Stanley Hauerwas, 'The Servant Community' in *The Hauerwas Reader*, edited by John Berkman and

Michael Cartwright (Durham, NC: Duke University Press, 2001), 381.

2 *Immortal, Invisible, God Only Wise*, written by Walter Chalmers Smith, a pastor of the Free Church of Scotland, in the late nineteenth century, and based on 1 Timothy 1.17.

3 Mayeul de Dreuille OSB, *The Rule of Saint Benedict and the Ascetic Traditions from Asia to the West*, translated with the collaboration of Mark Hargreaves OSB (Leominster: Gracewing, 2000), 333.

4 Michael Casey OCSO and David Tomlins OCSO, *Introducing Benedict's Rule: A Program of Formation* (Erzabtei St Ottilien: EOS, 2006), 90.

5 *The Rule of Saint Benedict*, edited and translated by Bruce L. Venarde (Cambridge, MA: Harvard University Press, 2011), 9.

6 Michael Paternoster, *Counsels for all Christians: Obedience, Stability and Conversion in the Rule of St Benedict* (Fairacres: SLG Press, 1980), 8.

7 Jürgen Moltmann, 'God in the World – the World in God' in *The Gospel of John and Christian Theology*, edited by Richard Bauckham and Carl Mosser (Grand Rapids MI: Eerdmans, 2008), 378.

8 Moltmann 2008, 379.

9 See http://daytoncastleman.com/artwork/2524835_Caravan.html, accessed April 2012.

10 Moltmann 2008, 380.

11 Moltmann 2008, 380.

12 Nicholas Boyle, 'Hegel and "The End of History"' in *New Blackfriars* 76:891 (1995), 115.

13 Boyle 1995, 116.

14 Boyle 1995, 117.

15 I am grateful to Edward Dowler for making this point, and indebted to him in the exploration of it which follows.

Chapter Six

1   Gregory of Nyssa, *Life of Macrina*, http://www. fordham.edu/halsall/basis/macrina.asp, accessed April 2012. Source: Gregory of Nyssa, *The Life of Macrina*, translated by W. K. Lowther Clarke (London: SPCK, 1916).

2   Natalie Carnes, *Senses of Beauty* (forthcoming book, 2013), 265–6. I am indebted in a number of ways to Carnes's wonderfully subtle readings of the *Life of Macrina*.

Chapter Seven

1   John Milbank, *The Word Made Strange: Theology, Language, Culture* (Oxford: Blackwell, 1997), 219–32.

2   William Blake, *I Heard an Angel*, ll.11–12.

3   Paul Tillich, *The Courage To Be*, 2nd edn (New Haven and London: Yale University Press, 2000), 3.

4   Tillich 2000, 43; my emphasis.

5   Milbank 1997, 228.

6   I am grateful to Michael Banner for this suggestion, and the discussion that follows from it.

7   Thomas L. Brodie, *The Gospel According to John: A Literary and Theological Commentary* (Oxford: Oxford University Press, 1993), 158–9.

8   See, for example, Richard Bauckham, 'The Fourth Gospel as the Testimony of the Beloved Disciple' in *The Gospel of John and Christian Theology*, edited by Richard Bauckham and Carl Mosser (Grand Rapids, MI: Eerdmans, 2008), 133–4.

9   Bauckham 2008, 134.

10 Rudolf Bultmann, *The Gospel of John: A Commentary*, translated by G. R. Beasley-Murray, R. W. N. Hoare and J. K. Riches (Oxford: Blackwell, 1971), 535–6.

Epilogue

1   To which we might add the one from Malachi 3.2 that Handel made so memorable with his musical setting of it in *Messiah*: 'But who may abide the day of his coming?'

2   Philip Pullman, *The Amber Spyglass* (London: Scholastic Press, 2000), 334–6.

3   Gregory of Nyssa, *Life of Macrina*, http://www.fordham.edu/halsall/basis/macrina.asp, accessed April 2012. Source: Gregory of Nyssa, *The Life of Macrina*, translated by W. K. Lowther Clarke, (London: SPCK, 1916).

4   John Ruskin, *Fors Clavigera: Letters to the Workmen and Labourers of Great Britain* (London: George Allen, 1896), 55.

5   My discussion of John 14.2 is indebted to conversation with David Ford, who is currently working on a theological commentary on John's Gospel.